At home with Flowers

At home with Flowers

Compiled by Coral Walker

LONGMEADOW
PRESS

A NOTE TO READERS
The publishers would like to advise you that
some flowers featured in this book may cause
an allergic response in a very limited number
of individuals. In the unlikely event of this
happening, we suggest you consult a doctor.

CREDITS
Flower Designs by: Jan Hall,
Mary Lawrence, Jane Newdick, Judy Taylor
and Sarah Waterkeyn

Consultants: Mary Lawrence, David Squire

Photographers: Di Lewis, Richard Paines,
Helen Pask and Steve Tanner

Managing Editor: Jilly Glassborow

Color Separation by:
Scantrans Pte Ltd., Singapore.

CONTENTS

$\mathscr{I}$NTRODUCTION

Over the years, much has been written about the beauty of flowers and the pleasure they bring. Anyone interested in growing, displaying or preserving flowers will already know just how satisfying it is to work with them, and how they can enhance every home and almost every occasion.

$\mathscr{A}$*t Home With Flowers* has been compiled as a comprehensive, informative and inspirational tool for the flower lover, whether a seasoned old-timer or someone new to the delights of all things floral. It endeavours to explore the versatility of flowers: to capture their fast-fading beauty and make the very best of all their properties.

In each chapter there is a wide variety of colourfully illustrated projects, which have simple explanations, and there are also full instructions on any techniques, materials and equipment you might need.

Fresh flowers are presented in a wide variety of ways, with designs that can be copied or used to gain inspiration. There is also a full guide to conditioning and caring for different flower types on pages 148-151 which will enable you to keep fresh blooms as long as possible.

There are three chapters devoted to preserved flowers — dried, pressed and pot-pourri — plus full information on preservation methods and fabulous decorations, recipes, designs and gifts you can make. *Flowers for Beauty* uses the healing and medicinal properties of plants in a number of easy-to-follow recipes for making your own beauty preparations, while the exotic and edible qualities of many flowers are explored in *Flowers as Food*.

Once you've tried your hand at some of these techniques and ideas, you might want to use them to give as presents. *Floral Gifts* has a large selection of floral presents to make for everyone.

Finally, we list popular flowers to grow in an easy-to-follow chart and give a guide to their best use. In most cases throughout the book, the plants are referred to by their common names with alternative American names given in brackets where necessary. However, a full list on page 166 gives both the common name in addition to the botanical name for easy reference.

Like flowers themselves, there is something in *At Home With Flowers* to please everyone. Whether it is used occasionally or often it makes wonderful browsing and helps to demonstrate that, indeed, the beauty of flowers and the joy they can bring, transcends fads, fashion and time.

A frosted glass vase in pale mauve is the perfect foil for fresh lavender. Later you can use the flowerheads for pot-pourri.

FRESH FLOWERS

Revel in the rich variety of shades and textures that fresh flowers have to offer.

Little can surpass that special quality of fresh flowers. Their transient charm, soon to fade, delights us all. How these lovely blooms and stems are put together needs few – if any – rules. From a lavishly arranged display to a handful of plucked garden flowers, the following chapter is crammed with arrangements, inspiration and tips to make the very best of freshly cut flowers.

 8

To get the most from fresh flowers it is worth following a few guidelines. These tips will ensure that whether you gather your blooms from the garden, or buy them from a florist or market stall, they will open into fully fledged beauty and last as long as possible.

Full details on buying, cutting and caring for fresh flowers and advice on the tools and mechanics of flower arranging appear on pages 148-151.

CONDITIONING

Always buy or pick flowers in peak condition. To keep them this way you should always condition them before setting them into any arrangement.

Generally, flowers bought from a florist will have been conditioned before they are sold, so they will only need their stems re-cut and a long, cool drink.

Pick garden flowers in the early morning, or toward evening when water loss is at its lowest and the plant is well charged with food. Cut the stems at an angle with a sharp knife or pair of scissors, place immediately into a bucket of tepid water and leave for several hours. Tough or woody stems will need to be slit upwards with a sharp knife. Particularly stubborn stems and those of shrubs will need crushing

ABOVE: One of the best times to pick flowers is in the early evening when they are fully charged with food and water.

with a hammer. All this enables the plant to absorb the maximum amount of water.

It is also best to strip all the lower leaves from the stems, as these not only deprive the flowerheads of water, but they will rot underwater and consequently will encourage bacteria to grow.

TOOLS AND EQUIPMENT

Garden scissors, secateurs, and a sharp knife are all useful for preparing flowers.

For arrangements, it is worth investing in a few mechanics to support the flowers. These include fresh florists' foam (the green variety) which comes in a range of shapes and sizes; it can be cut down as necessary and needs to be well soaked before use. Alternatively, wire mesh can be crumpled into the base of a vase or container.

Pin holders (also known as florists' foam anchor spikes) are cast lead blocks covered with brass pins. Pin holders are useful for shallow arrangements. The flower stems are pushed on to the pins, which hold them in place. Lightweight plastic prongs are used in conjunction with florists' putty for holding foam in place. Florists' adhesive tape is also useful for securing foam to a plate or awkwardly shaped container.

BELOW: Tough stems can be conditioned by cutting two upward slits in them with a sharp knife.

BELOW: Help woody stems to absorb water more easily by crushing their ends with a heavy object like a hammer.

Yellow

Yellow-green

Yellow-orange

Green

Orange

Blue-green

Ornage-red

Blue

Red

Blue-violet

Red-violet

Violet

FLOWER DESIGN

There are no longer any hard and fast rules to arranging flowers. The stiff, contrived styles of the 1950s have been superseded by much less formal displays that use simple lines, more monochrome (one colour) and a wide array of unusual containers.

However, it is still worth taking a look at a few standard design principles before you begin. Basically, you need to consider outline, balance and harmony.

The outline, or shape, of the arrangement depends largely on the flowers you are using. The tallest flowers usually establish the height, the boldest blooms form the

LEFT: The cream and lilac of these roses and sweet peas are a perfect complement.

focal point, or centre, of the display, while smaller blooms and foliage can fill in gaps and add depth to the display.

The angle from which the arrangement is to be seen will also affect the shape of the finished display. Will it be seen from all sides or only face on? Is it for a table centrepiece? In this case it should be low lying so that dinner guests can see over it.

Balance need not mean formality. But a well-balanced display will not appear either top-heavy or lop-sided. It will also be well proportioned: you would hardly put a few small fragile sweet peas into a huge, dramatic container — the balance would be totally wrong.

Harmony covers colour and setting. Look at the colours. Do they contrast or are they toning and from the same area of the colour spectrum? (See the colour wheel above.)

ABOVE: This wheel is a guide to colour harmony. Warm colours (red, yellow, orange) sit on one side of the wheel while the cool colours (blue, violet, green) are on the other. Complementary colours are those opposite each other on the wheel.

What container are you using and where are you setting the display? A small posy would be lost in a large room, for example.

You should also think about lighting. Will the display be seen in natural daylight or will it be picked out by an electric light, such as a table lamp or spotlight?

In the end, flower design, like any other art form, is largely subjective. What appeals to one person may not necessarily attract another. Do not feel restricted; experimenting as much as you can is half the enjoyment of this pleasurable pastime.

EXOTIC MEDLEY

Orange lilies
Pink 'Stargazer' lilies
Pink larkspur
Nasturtiums
Bright pink pelargoniums
Pale yellow and mid pink alstroemeria
Garden marigolds
Onion heads
Pink roses
African daisies
Deep magenta carnations
Selection of jugs

The inspiration for this exotic fantasy is a richly patterned tablecloth with leaves, flowers and birds. A group of vases filled with vivid blooms such as these would make a perfect decoration for an evening buffet or garden party.

The flowers are very simply arranged, relying on the fusion of bright, clashing colours and strong contours.

Here, the strong orange in the tablecloth has been picked as the basic colour for the display, and orange lilies make a bold start in the larger green jug. Mix them with several pink lilies, a couple of pink roses and place a few long stems of larkspur to the back of the jug.

The round, pink vase contains a handful or two of orange nasturtiums, shocking-pink pelargoniums and pinkish alstroemeria. The neighbouring vase has a mixture of alstroemeria, marigolds and some more of the orange lilies.

The smaller of the two green jugs holds most of the lily blooms, this time combined with onion heads, roses, pelargoniums, carnations and daisies.

This Exotic Medley of rich colours takes its inspiration from the boldly patterned table cover. The result is almost tropical.

ABOVE: Rich red ranunculus and pale green bells of Ireland provide a soft, velvet texture.

RED VELVET

*Bells of Ireland
Garlic flowerheads
White statice
Summer cypress (Kochia scoparia)
Pink scabious (pincushion flowers)
Red ranunculus
Laurustinus
Water jug and bowl
Florists' foam*

An old water jug and bowl provide the perfect setting for this traditional arrangement, with its bold colours and contours.

Wedge left-over scraps of soaked foam into the jug. Then position a few large stems of bells of Ireland with two or three garlic flowerheads to establish the height and outline. Fill in the outline with the summer cypress and statice, keeping the stems at least 2in (5cm) shorter than the garlic and bells of Ireland. Then add the scabious throughout the display.

Brilliant red ranunculus instantly lift the arrangement, their colour and texture a striking contrast to the existing plants. To finish the display, tuck in a few stems of flowering laurustinus.

Laurustinus
Eucalyptus
Red spray carnations and buds
Shiny kitchen bakeware
Florists' foam
Silver paint spray

The kitchen is often the first place to look for useful and attractive containers. Pretty aluminium cases, such as the ones that have been used in this arrangement, are shiny and create attractive highlights.

First, spray some longer stems of eucalyptus with silver spray paint. Make sure that you do this in a well-ventilated room — paint fumes can be quite toxic if they are inhaled. Leave the eucalyptus to dry on a piece of newspaper. It will not take long, and in the meantime you can begin building up the display.

Place a piece of soaked florists' foam in the baking case, then create the outline of the arrangement with some long stems of laurustinus. Once the eucalyptus is dry, slot it in among the laurustinus.

Use the carnations to form the focal point of the display and fill in any gaps with carnation buds and flowers. Finally, for depth, recess some dark red laurustinus buds.

HARVEST GARLAND

Ripe ears of wheat
Field poppies (fresh or artificial), or common marigolds
Chamomile flowers
Cornflowers
Florists' foam ring
Florists' wire

Harvest festival garlands are so often made from dried flowers, so this fresh one makes a delightful change. However, fresh poppies do not last very long so you may

ABOVE: This Harvest Garland has been made from ripe ears of wheat, poppies, cornflowers and chamomile.

choose to use artificial ones instead.

Soak the foam ring well and build up the garland with the wheat, ensuring that the ears follow the same direction. Tuck in the cornflowers fairly evenly around the garland and add the chamomile flowers. Finish with the bright red poppies or, for a longer lasting display, you can use common or pot marigolds instead.

ABOVE: These bright and shiny baking tins make great containers for silver-sprayed foliage and bright blooms.

SCARLET ANEMONES

Red anemones
Marguerite foliage
Small-headed asters (September flowers)
Colander or round bowl
Saucer
Florists' foam
Florists' tape
Florists' putty

Brilliant scarlet anemones dominate this lovely arrangement, which nestles in an old-fashioned enamelled colander. You could use any round bowl or dish.

First, tape a piece of soaked florists' foam to a saucer and secure it inside the colander with a little putty.

Cover the foam with feathery marguerite foliage and form the dome-shaped outline for the other flowers. Follow this rounded

ABOVE: Create a cheerful display with brilliant red anemones and tiny asters.

design with the anemones, positioning them so that their faces look up and out.

Offset the deep reds and greens of the anemones and the marguerite foliage with sprays of asters, tucking them in throughout the arrangement.

 15

LILY BOUQUET

Lilies (Lilium longiflorum)
Snowball flowers (Viburnum opulus)
Iris or gladioli leaves
Florists' wire

The strong, uncluttered shape and heady fragrance of *Lilium longiflorum* makes it an ideal flower for a wedding bouquet.

This bouquet is a simple sheaf and is very easily constructed. It is designed to be carried resting over one arm, with the stems supported by the opposite hand.

Begin by stripping the lower leaves from the stems of the snowball flowers. You can strengthen the heavy flowerheads by using a fine silver wire.

Then take the first lily in one hand to determine the length of the bouquet. With the other hand begin to build up the bouquet, gathering the lilies and snowball flowers and placing them so that the heads graduate down toward the handhold.

When you are happy with the shape, bind wire firmly around the stems, just under the lowest flowerheads, and trim the stems to the same length. Cover the wire with long, narrow iris or gladioli leaves.

OPEN BOX

Common or English laurel
Yellow double tulips
Cream spider chrysanthemums
Cream coloured lilies
Wooden box
Twig
Plate
Florists' foam
Florists' tape

Bring out the warm sheen of a lovely wooden box by filling it with lustrous laurel leaves and creamy-yellow flowerheads.

LEFT: The large white trumpet lilies in this striking sheaf make a beautiful bouquet for the modern bride.

Tape soaked florists' foam to a plate before inserting it into the box. Now prop open the box lid with a small twig.

Create the outline of the arrangement with the laurel, covering the foam and filling the open box. Next, cut the tulips on the slant so that they slot into the foam more easily. Keep them the same length and position them throughout the display. Push in the spider chrysanthemums to add depth and contrast, and finish off with the focal flowers, the lilies.

YELLOW TRIO

Gerbera
Foliage
Yellow broom
Cocktail shaker
Florists' foam

ABOVE: A profusion of lilies, tulips and laurel tumble out of this old wooden box.

A cocktail shaker doubles up as a vase for this highly effective yet simple arrangement. Put a piece of soaked florists' foam into the shaker base, then insert three gerbera flowers, graduating the length of the stems. Add just a little foliage (in this case carnation foliage) behind and in front of the second tallest gerbera.

Position some curving sprays of yellow broom on either side of the display. The spiky flowers of the broom contrast with the soft petals of the gerbera.

Reserve some short stems of broom and insert these into a small piece of soaked florists' foam which has been postioned in the shaker lid. To complete the effect, place this at the base of the main arrangement.

BELOW: With only three main flowers, Yellow Trio proves how effective a simple design can be.

SPRING CHORUS

Daffodils and leaves
Forget-me-nots
Straw basket
Plastic container to fit inside basket
Wire mesh

A wicker basket provides a country setting for this charming display of spring daffodils and early forget-me-nots. Before starting your display, line the basket with a plastic container to protect it and fill this with crushed wire mesh.

Position a bunch of daffodils at the back of the container, adding daffodil leaves to give a natural look. Then group the forget-me-nots into several small bunches and insert them throughout the basket, tucking some into the front so that they just peep over the edge.

Finally, cut down the remaining daffodils and position these at random among the forget-me-not bunches to complete this picturesque country display.

SPRINGTIME POSY

White lilac
Blue hyacinths
Pale yellow roses
Yellow freesia
Paper doily
Rubber band or florists' wire twist
Glue
Ribbon (optional)

Posies are simple to put together, yet the finished results are so satisfying.

First, condition the lilac by standing the stripped short stems in 2in (5cm) of boiling water for two minutes, then give them a cool drink for several hours. Gather all the flowers into a bunch, trim the stems to the same length and then bind the posy with a florists' wire twist or rubber band.

Cut to the centre of the doily, and cut out enough of the centre to accommodate the flowers. Wrap the doily around the posy and overlap the edges, securing them with a little glue. Finish off with some ribbon.

ABOVE: This attractive, scented posy, easily assembled, would be sure to delight any recipient.

AMETHYST ARRAY

Larkspur (Delphinium elatum)
Bouvardia
Alstroemeria
Traditional salt jar
Florists' foam

In this attractive arrangement, gently flowing lines and contours have been created with just three varieties of flowers. And the ceramic salt jar — with its 'open mouth' — provides the perfect backdrop.

First, wedge a piece of soaked foam into the mouth of the jar. Then form a gently curving horizontal line with the larkspur. Push a little bouvardia into the jar to provide some depth to the arrangement and finish off with the alstroemeria as the focal flowers, allowing a few longer stems to protrude and strengthen the outline.

LEFT: A country-style basket is packed with spring forget-me-nots and daffodils.

ABOVE: Amethyst-blue larkspur set the scene for clusters of alstroemeria.

 19

HERBAL BOUQUET

Mixed flowering herbs such as:
chives, mint, chicory,
winter savory, hyssop, rosemary,
thyme, lemon balm, lavender,
feverfew, tansy and rue
Glass tank

There comes a point in mid-summer when most shrubby herbs have spikes of flowers on them. Subtle and unassuming, these flowers look well in cosy jugs and plain glass shapes, and make the perfect accompaniment to the kitchen dresser or table.

Collect as many flowering herbs as you can. Any of the herbs listed above are suitable. Half fill the tank with water. Strip most of the lower leaves off the plants and group the flowers in bunches in a country style arrangement.

This is also a highly practical display — you can easily pick the odd leaf or two when you are cooking to flavour a soup or perk up a salad.

AMARYLLIS IN MARBLES

Amaryllis (Hippeastrum)
Oblong glass tank
Green glass marbles

BELOW: Marbles serve as an attractive support for flowers in glass. Here, they play a principal role in a display of red amaryllis.

Simplicity itself, this modern design relies on straight lines and bold colours to create a striking effect.

Half fill a glass tank with marbles and carefully cover them with water. Cut three stems of amaryllis — two of similar length and one slightly longer — and push these into the marbles. The hollow stems will curl in the water, so the marbles are excellent for holding them in position. Place the two shorter amaryllis on one side of the vase, with the other on the opposite side.

SCARLET AND PURPLE

Scarlet, pink and orange ranunculus
Blue irises
Red parrot tulips
Bluebells
Blue hyacinths
Forget-me-nots
Clematis
Eucalyptus
Vase

ABOVE: Flowering herbs have a simplicity and subtlety of colour not often exploited in flower arrangements.

RIGHT: A brilliant and daring mix of scarlet and purple flowers set in a simple vase makes a stunning arrangement.

Jewel-bright colours make this a striking but informal arrangement. The vase will easily support the flowers and no mechanics are needed.

Begin at the back of the vase with irises and eucalyptus to form a soft, symmetrical backdrop. Then in front of these add a few shorter stemmed tulips.

Now add a dense mass of bright ranunculus to form the central part of the display. To offset all the reds, tuck in some bluebells and pale blue hyacinths — beautiful for a heady scent — and, to finish off, insert an occasional forget-me-not and some pieces of trailing clematis.

BUTTERY YELLOW

Yellow and apricot coloured roses
Lady's mantle
Shallow bowl
Wire mesh

Little can match the beauty of full-blown garden roses, and a pretty lustre bowl with a gilt base is ideal for this rich mix of buttery yellow and soft peach.

Crumple the wire mesh and push it into the bowl. Fill with water. Cut the stems of the roses quite short so that the flowers sit close to the bowl. Push each one into the mesh until you have an even dome shape.

Finally, tuck in some sprays of acid green lady's mantle to offset the roses and bring the whole display to life.

LEFT: A golden lustre bowl is filled with buttery yellow roses and green lady's mantle.

BELOW: Lofty delphiniums create a magnificent floor-standing display.

ABOVE: Put a redundant goldfish bowl to good use with this eye-catching arrangement.

DELPHINIUM BLUE

Delphiniums
Yellow antirrhinums
Blue/mauve hydrangeas
Large vase
Wire mesh
Florists' tape

Choose a tall, sturdy vase and bold, elegant flowers to create a stunning floor-standing arrangement which will complement any sitting room or hallway.

Loosely pack the vase with the crumpled wire mesh. Bend a circle of wire mesh to overlap the rim of the vase and secure it in place with florists' tape. Then fill the vase with water.

Place the tallest delphinium in the centre of the vase. Position the others in front and to the side of the central stem, graduating the flowers downward in height to create a well-balanced effect.

Intersperse the delphiniums with antirrhinums, following the line of the design. To complete, form a collar of hydrangea blooms around the neck of the vase.

SEASCAPE

Gypsophila (baby's breath)
Brodiaea
Peach spray carnations
Dried onion heads
Goldfish bowl
Seashells and pebbles

A goldfish bowl and seashells form the setting for this attractive and unusual free-flowing arrangement. First, fill the bowl carefully with a mixture of shells and pebbles before adding the water.

The aim is to achieve a 'waterspray' effect with the first few flowers. Start with gypsophila (baby's breath), trailing a little over the side. Next add stems of delicate blue *Brodiaea*, following the same outline.

Peach spray carnations reflect the colour in some of the seashells and only a few are needed to follow the sweeping outline that you have already established. Dried onion heads have a lovely texture and their colour is picked up by the pebbles and shells. Place eight or so throughout the arrangement, filling in the outline.

White 'Iceberg' roses
Poppy seedheads
White water jug and bowl

'Iceberg' roses have a freshness and simplicity that few blooms can match. They demand a simple treatment, too, to achieve the best effect.

First fill the jug with water and then add a good bunchful of the roses, keeping some

GARLAND IN WHITE

White gladioli
Chervil
Cow parsley (alternatively, meadow parsley or
wild carrot)
White chrysanthemums
Rue
Variegated geranium foliage
Eucalyptus
Poppy and flax seedheads
Florists' foam ring

This lovely garland is made from shades of cream, green and white. It provides welcome relief from heavier, winter displays.

ABOVE: 'Iceberg' roses tumble from a graceful plain white jug and bowl and combine well with the aqua-silver of poppy seedheads.

Soak the foam ring well and begin making the garland by inserting the eucalyptus and other foliage in clusters. Next, add groups of chervil and cow parsley. Tuck in two or three chrysanthemum flowerheads and poppy and flax seedheads. Finally, work round the garland with the principal flowers — the gladioli.

Keep all the stems short and condition the rue and the wildflowers overnight before you use them.

of them upright, allowing others to nod gently over the edge of the jug. Intersperse the arrangement with poppy seedheads; you will find that their natural silvery blue hue makes the perfect match.

Finish off with a few roses resting in a little water in the bowl.

BELOW: White gladioli and chrysanthemums, combined with variegated foliage in shades of cream and green, create a serene effect.

ABOVE: Cool shades of green foliage and glass create a tranquil display.

TRANQUILLITY

Bear grass
Birds of paradise leaves
Bells of Ireland
Leucodendron foliage
Snow-on-the-mountain
Green glass jugs or tankards
Green marbles

This serene display uses only shades of green to achieve the tranquil effect.

To begin, place marbles in the bottom of the larger jug and half fill the jug with water. Then build up the basic outline with bear grass, allowing the blades to curve out on either side. Use birds of paradise leaves in the centre of the grass.

Add two stems of bells of Ireland next, one slightly shorter than the other, then fill out the display with *Leucodendron* foliage. Finish off the arrangement with a few pieces of variegated snow-on-the-mountain at the front.

The smaller jug holds only a clump of snow-on-the-mountain and, set as it is next to its larger counterpart, it completes the picture beautifully.

ORIENTAL BLOSSOM

Sprays of apple blossom
Pink tulips
Chinese-style bowl
Large metal pinholder
Florists' foam

The natural simplicity and freshness of flowering apple blossom combined with pale pink tulips adds a timeless tranquillity to this Oriental setting. A Chinese bowl gives a touch of authenticity.

Use a large metal pinholder in the bottom of the bowl to act as a balance and fill the bowl with well-soaked florists' foam.

Strip the bark from the lower stems of the apple branches and crush them well with a hammer to aid water absorption.

Position two branches at the back of the bowl at an oblique angle. Place shorter branches at the front of the bowl at the same angle. Put one more branch at the front of the bowl, positioning it so that it bends down to touch the table.

Starting from the left, and following the line of the final branch, position the tulips to create a central focal point.

RIGHT: The lines of this minimalist display are taken from the Oriental style of flower arrangement.

DUET FOR PEONIES

Pink peonies
Blue cornflowers
Eucalyptus foliage
Matching jugs
String

The floral design on these pretty blue and pink patterned jugs is beautifully complemented by the choice of peonies and cornflowers. You will need at least 20 peonies — both open and in bud — although it will depend upon the size of your jugs.

The main display in the larger of the two jugs is bunched and tied with string before it is put into the container. This slightly more unusual type of flower arrangement, often known as a hostess bunch, provides a good alternative to using florists' foam.

Arrange a fan shape of eucalyptus in one hand and secure this with string. Bind the peonies firmly into the bunch, following the shape of the eucalyptus and adding in extra budding peonies, open peonies and foliage as you work.

Next add a flourish of cornflowers down one side of the jug and finish the arrange-

LEFT: Multi-petalled peonies make wonderful, rich displays. These pretty pale pink peonies are offset by the deep blue of the cornflowers.

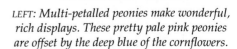 

ment with a short bunch at the base of the display. Firmly secure the bunch with more string and insert it into the jug.

For the arrangement in the smaller jug, cut down some peonies so that the heads sit neatly into the rim of the jug. To finish off, position a few of the cornflowers in the centre of the display.

Make sure that you keep the water levels in the jugs topped up so that the flowers last for as long as possible.

BELOW: The bold, sunny faces of coral-pink gerbera form the focal point of this traditional display.

PINK GERBERA

Eucalyptus
Small-headed asters (September flowers)
Pink gladioli
White and blue delphiniums
Pink gerbera
White spray chrysanthemums
Bells of Ireland
Vase

Originally from South Africa, gerbera are now widely available internationally as cut flowers. Their bold flowerheads and wonderful array of colours make them the ideal focal point for any display.

Fill the vase with water and build up the outline using eucalyptus and some small-headed asters. (These little daisy-type flowers are often known as September flowers in Britain.) Curve the eucalyptus down toward the base of the display and position the feathery asters upright at the back.

Add to the outline by inserting a few short stems of gladioli, then fill in with white and blue delphiniums.

Now position the gerbera, keeping them to the foreground of the display and allowing one to drape over the front of the vase. Recess a few chrysanthemums and finish off with two or three stems of bells of Ireland for an interesting textural contrast.

ABOVE: The pink and peach blooms of roses and carnations nestle in a pretty glass bowl.

PINK AND PEACH ROSE BOWL

Pink/peach floribunda roses
Deep peach carnations
Paler peach carnations
Variegated ivy
Posy bowl
Florists' foam

Old-fashioned pink glass makes an ideal setting for this pleasing arrangement.

Fill the bowl with soaked florists' foam. Place the ivy leaves around the edge, overlapping them a little. To establish the height of the display, measure a single rosebud stem against the bowl — it should be the height of the container plus a third. Position this rose in the centre of the bowl and add the remaining roses, turning the bowl as you work to create an even effect.

Fill in with carnations, taking care not to overlap the ivy leaves. Tuck in a few more ivy leaves throughout the display.

ROSE BASKET

Selection of old-fashioned garden roses such as
'Baron Girod L'Ain', 'Celeste',
Rosa gallica 'Officinalis' or 'Fantin Latour'
Wicker basket with handle
Florists' foam
Polythene or plastic bag

Full-blown early summer roses capture the look of a Fantin-Latour painting. The many-petalled blooms are richly perfumed and softly coloured, and anything else with them would spoil their perfection.

Line the basket with polythene, and pack it with well-soaked florists' foam. Make sure the roses have been well conditioned and the lower leaves have been stripped off (see page 9). Then insert them into the basket, fairly randomly, making sure that the whole display is no higher than the handle.

RIGHT: A selection of old-fashioned roses in a rustic basket brings a wonderfully fragrant touch of the countryside into the home.

SWEEPING FERN

Sprengeri fern (Asparagus sprengeri)
Creamy-pink alstroemeria
White lilac
Pink daisy chrysanthemums
Tall vase

A tall, curving vase sets the style for this elegant, sweeping arrangement. Put only water into the vase as the narrow neck will support the display.

Take a few long stems of fern, positioning some upright and curving one large piece so that it sweeps down in front of the vase. Then add two long stems and one shorter one of alstroemeria.

Create a central column by using white lilac; this will give depth to the display. Finally, take stems of chrysanthemums in graduating lengths and place them throughout the arrangement.

BELOW: Soft curving lines of feathery fern sweep down from a profusion of sugary-pink and cream blooms.

ABOVE: A miniature potted tree is easy to assemble from shiny leaves and rosebuds.

FRESH FLOWER TREE

Small evergreen leaves such as camellia tips,
laurustinus, or Mexican orange
Large rosebuds
Terracotta pot and saucer
Soil
Small straight branch
Florists' foam brick
Wet florists' foam sphere

Miniature trees made from leaves and flowers make charming displays, particularly if used in pairs.

Tightly pack an old terracotta pot with florists' foam and push in a straight stick or small branch. Wedge a well-soaked foam sphere on to the top of the stick.

Insert the foliage into the sphere, turning the pot as you work to keep an even shape.

Cut the stems of the roses fairly short — while necessary for this design, it will also enable the water to reach the flowerheads. Tuck the rosebuds in among the leaves and finish with some soil around the base to cover the foam.

The woody stems of the shrubs and roses will need to be well conditioned before inserting them into this display. This will ensure that the plants last as long as possible. (For conditioning tips, see page 9).

IVY SWAG WITH LILIES

Glossy ivy
White lilies (Lilium longiflorum
and Lilium 'Mont Blanc')
Artificial fruit or berries
Small tray
Reel wire
Florists' foam
Masking tape or drawing pins
Red cord

This stunning swag is made simply from trailing ivy. It is offset with a glorious display of white lilies, which are perfect for a special occasion.

Begin by forming the swag. Measure out a piece of red cord the length you wish the swag to be. Using reel wire, secure the ivy along the cord, joining short pieces of ivy together with more wire as necessary.

The swag can then be looped along a mantelpiece, above a doorway or across a piece of furniture such as a buffet table. Secure it with masking tape or pins. You can wire in pieces of artificial fruit for a more bountiful effect.

For the lily arrangement, tape a brick of soaked florists' foam to a tray. Trim and clean more of the glossy green ivy foliage and use it to cover the foam. Tuck in the smaller lilies and the lily buds. Use the *Lilium longiflorum* blooms to form the focal point of the display.

RIGHT: Loops of glossy green ivy contrast with pure white lilies.

DUTCH MASTER

Delphiniums
Poppies
Cornflowers
Yellow knapweed (globe centaurea)
Roses
Foxgloves
Peonies
Daylilies (Hemerocallis)
Yarrow
Scabious (pincushion flower)
Love-in-a-mist
Alstroemeria
Mallow
White 'Alba' gladioli
Pinks (Dianthus x allwoodii)
Urn
Florists' foam

The richly detailed flower paintings of the 17th and 18th centuries can be recreated in your home in early summer when there is an abundance of flowers. This arrangement faces only one way, so place it against a wall. Choose flowers which have long, straight stems, in vivid colours with as near perfect blooms as possible.

First soak the foam well and pack it into the urn. This is a traditional triangular display, so begin by creating the outline. Use the longest-stemmed blooms — for example, the delphiniums — starting at the back of the display to provide the height and working down each side, keeping the line fairly symmetrical.

Mix the colours daringly, and work down the arrangement and out toward the sides with spiky gladioli, alstroemeria, mallow, cornflowers and love-in-a-mist.

Use the larger blooms — roses, poppies, daylilies and scabious — to fill the centre of the display and form the focal point.

Fill in any gaps with buds and remaining flowers. A little trailing foliage, such as honeysuckle, adds a touch of panache.

LEFT: The exquisite flower paintings of the 17th and 18th centuries provide an excellent source of ideas for flower arrangers today.

PRIMARY COLOURS

Variegated Pittosporum foliage
Gypsophila (baby's breath)
Yellow lilies
Holly berries (English holly)
Shallow blue glass bowl
Wire mesh

So often, it is the container that dictates the flowers you use. Here, the deep blue glass of this attractive 1930s bowl is offset by the bold yellows and reds of the flowers and berries, giving the whole display a striking note of primary colours.

First, make sure that the *Pittosporum* and holly (English holly) foliage has been well conditioned, otherwise it will deteriorate long before the rest of the display. Hammer the stems well and give them a long drink of water. (If you have trouble finding twigs with real berries, you can always cheat and use artificial ones.)

Squash the mesh into the bowl and fill it with water. Keeping a shallow outline, fill the bowl with stems of bushy *Pittosporum*. Intersperse stems of gypsophila (baby's breath) throughout the arrangement to relieve the density of the foliage.

Create the focal point with three open lilies, also adding a few buds.

Finally, position several twiggy pieces of holly, bearing as many berries as possible, throughout the display.

Bright blue glassware has inspired the use of primary colours and bold contours in this attractive display.

DRIED FLOWER DESIGNS

*When new, dried flowers have almost all the
vivid colour and strong form of their
fresh counterparts.*

Dried flowers are versatile, long-lasting and – if
preserved carefully – can retain the richness of
colour and beauty of form that they enjoy when
fresh. On the following pages, discover the best
way to preserve flowers and be inspired by dozens
of wonderfully different displays.

*I*n recent years the popularity of dried flowers has soared as the variety and availability of plant material has increased one-hundred fold. Specialist shops and an increasing number of florists now stock a wide variety of dried flowers, leaves and seedheads imported from all over the world.

But don't feel you have to buy all your dried material. Preserving your own can be immensely satisfying and enjoyable and the results can be as professional as anything you can buy in a shop.

BUYING DRIED FLOWERS

When buying dried flowers, make sure they are not dusty, dull specimens left over from the previous year. The best time to buy is in the autumn, soon after the fresh flower's natural season. Obviously, some flowers, and certainly leaves and seedheads, last very well. To check, make sure the colours are quite bright and not too faded, that the flower's foliage is a dull green and not a washed out grey and that none of the material is brittle or crumbling.

PRESERVING YOUR OWN

If you haven't a garden, try growing plants in patio tubs or window boxes. Or preserve bought fresh flowers. Market stalls are good places to buy inexpensive fresh flowers and many can be dried.

The cardinal rule is always to dry flowers in their prime. If you are picking garden flowers, choose a dry day just before the flowers are fully open and preferably in the middle of the day when the sap is rising. Shake off any dew and make sure that the petals are completely dry before you begin.

ABOVE: Yarrow – with its clusters of bright yellow flowers – is an easy plant to grow and it dries well.

LEFT: Always pick flowers in their prime. Choose a dry day and make sure the petals are free from dew or dampness. The best time for this is around midday

DRYING METHODS

There are several methods of preserving flowers but some plants can only successfully be dried by one method.

Air drying
One of the easiest drying methods is air drying. Many flowers can simply be left hanging upside down to dry in a dark, airy place such as an airing cupboard, attic or a spare room. It is important that the flowers are not put in direct sunlight as this will cause their colours to fade. You should first bind the flowers together in bunches before hanging them. Rubber bands are best for this purpose as you will find that the stems shrink as they dry.

Suspend the flowers from a pole or some string and leave them till they are thoroughly dry. Particularly check the top of the stem, just below the flowerhead, because if this isn't dried out the flower will quickly droop when stood upright.

Some plants, such as sea lavender and pampas grass, dry best standing upright in a vase or jam jar. Others, like hydrangea, need to stand in a little water while they dry. Grasses and some seedheads dry best lying flat on newspaper. It is a good idea

Many flowers can be dried successfully by hanging them upside down in a shaded, airy place. Keep them out of direct sunlight as this will fade their colours.

to spray bushy grasses with hair spray as they have a tendency to explode and scatter their seeds everywhere.

Plants to air dry: sea lavender, lavender, statice, roses, love-in-a-mist, gypsophila (baby's breath), lady's mantle, delphinium, all seedheads and grasses, bottlebrush, sunray (Helipterum), helichrysum (straw-flowers), Chinese lanterns and hops.

 36

Glycerine

Most foliage is preserved using glycerine. Basically, the glycerine replaces the water in the leaves leaving them supple and leathery. Choose fresh foliage during the summer when the sap is still rising.

Hammer woody stems well so that they absorb the glycerine solution. The solution should be made from one part glycerine to two parts very hot water. Stir it well and stand the leaf sprays in about 3in (7.5cm) of the solution. This method can take about 10 days to four weeks. Wipe the leaves with a damp cloth if they begin to 'sweat'. If the leaves appear to wither and not absorb the solution, cut the stems back and try again.

Single leaves can also be preserved with glycerine by immersing them in a small dish of the solution. This should only take two or three days to work.

Plants to preserve with glycerine: virtually all green foliage can be preserved this way. However, silvered, downy or hairy leaves do not 'glycerine' well.

Desiccants

Desiccants — or drying agents — draw moisture from the plant and help to preserve the natural colours and form.

One of the simplest to use is silica gel, which can be bought from most hardware stores or chemists. It usually comes in white or blue crystals. The blue crystals will turn pink when they have absorbed water, so you will know when the plants are ready.

Put a layer of crystals in an airtight container and place several flowerheads on top (daisy types — face down, others — face up). Gently spoon more crystals on top to cover the flowers. Tightly secure the lid. Leave the flowers for a couple of days, then check; the petals should feel like tissue when they are ready.

Borax is cheaper than silica gel but it takes around 10 days to work. Ideally, it

Provided flowers stay out of any steam, they dry well when suspended above a solid fuel range, which gives out constant warmth.

LEFT: Remember that texture and contrast are important in dried arrangements. Don't just dry flowers; artichoke heads and seed-heads can also be dried to add interest.

BASIC EQUIPMENT AND TECHNIQUES

Various items can be used to support dry flowers: florists' foam, specially designed for dry arrangements, is the most popular. It is grey in colour, comes in various shapes such as cones, tablets, spheres and bricks. and it can be cut easily to fit any container.

Wire mesh is also used to support larger displays. It can be crumpled or crushed into shape and packed with moss to form the base of a garland or pendant.

A variety of wire is used in dried flower arranging. Stub wires are straight lengths of wire used for supporting fragile flow-ers or binding small bunches of flowers together. They can also be used to support nuts and cones. Once wired, it is easy to insert these items into the foam base. Reel wire is finer and is used for more delicate work. U-pins are like wire hairpins and are used to attach various items into a display.

LEFT: Many flowers can be given the desic-cant treatment. A selection of perfect flower-heads lies in boxfuls of dessicant powder. More of the powder will be poured over and around each bloom before the lids are closed.

BELOW: You can give flowers more impact in a display by wiring them into small bunches before arranging them. First bend one end of a stub wire (a straight length of wire) into a hairpin or U-shape as shown.

BELOW: Cut the flower stems short and position them against the pin. Wind the long end of the wire about three times around the plant stems, then straighten it out to make a wire 'stem'.

should be mixed with dry silver sand: three parts borax to two parts sand. Cover the flowers as with silica gel. To speed up the process you can use a microwave oven. But do make sure you check with your manu-facturer's instructions beforehand. Cover the flowers with silica gel as before, but leave the container uncovered. Put it in the microwave oven together with a glass of water. Set to full power for 1-4 minutes depending on the fragility of the flower.

Flowers to preserve with desiccants: lily, cornflower, daffodil, daisy, freesia, pansy, hellebore, marigold, peony, rose and violet.

RIGHT: Decorative sprays of flowers and foliage combine with tartan ribbon to bring to life an ordinary picture frame.

TANSY IN TERRACOTTA

Tansy
Wheat
Yarrow
Deep blue larkspur
Lavender
Sea holly or eryngo (Eryngium)
Old terracotta flower pot

This informal arrangement, displayed in a lovely weathered old flower pot, needs no mechanics to secure it.

Use plenty of tansy to form a dense outline. Add the taller plants and long stems of wheat to the back of the display. Push some shorter stems of wheat into the foreground. Fill in any gaps with clusters of sea holly. (Tansy can cause dermatitis so it's advisable to take care when using it.)

ABOVE: This Kitchen Spice Ball – with its exotic textures and shapes – is made from a range of spices and seedheads.

LEFT: Tansies are one of the easiest flowers to preserve. Their stems stay stiff and their colours remain true.

KITCHEN SPICE BALL

Cinnamon sticks
Spanish root (liquorice sticks)
Star anise
White lomius
Small and large poppy seedheads
Cones
Florists' dry foam sphere
Raffia
Stub wire

This aromatic pomander contains a range of interesting spices and seedheads and makes an attractive kitchen decoration.

Begin by plaiting three strands of raffia to form a hanging loop. Wire this into the dry foam sphere.

Make little bundles of cinnamon sticks and Spanish root and bind them with wire. Cover the wire with raffia strands. Wire the star anise and the lomius and cover the sphere with all these ingredients, trying to keep the display roughly spherical.

Now insert groups of large and small poppy seedheads into the remaining gaps.

To finish off your spice ball, add a few dark cones to give depth and substance to the display. The ones we used here are platyspernum cones.

FRAMED WITH FLOWERS

Clubrush (bulrush)
Yellow crepis (hawkbeard)
Bottlebrush flowers and foliage
White leaf skeletons
Picture frame
Tartan ribbon
Round tablet of florists' dry foam
Florists' tape

This attractive design illustrates how much a dried floral arrangement can enhance a plain picture frame — it's easy to do but so very effective.

Begin by slicing the foam into two round pieces and then taping them to two corners of the frame. Next, using single stems of clubrush, build up a loose spray shape. For a splash of colour, tuck in stems of crepis or other yellow plant, allowing some to trail across the frame and picture. Then insert a number of single stems of bottlebrush.

Once the sprays are complete, fill them out with plenty of bottlebrush foliage. Add highlights with a few leaf skeletons.

The tartan ribbon adds the finishing touch to the arrangement. Make two double bows and wire them into the sprays, balancing each corner of the picture frame.

 41

LAVENDER SHEAF

Lavender
String or twine
Raffia or unbleached fabric ribbon

Lavender is such a delightful dried flower with its deep purple-blue colour and glorious aroma that sometimes it is best displayed just by itself.

To make a sheaf, you will need quite a lot of lavender for a generous effect. Gather the lavender into one hand, keeping all the flowerheads at the same level. Holding on tightly to the bunch with one hand, wrap a piece of twine or string around the stems and tie it in a secure knot. It is a great help if you can enlist another willing pair of hands at this stage.

Trim off the bottom of the stalks to the same length and cover the twine with raffia or ribbon, finishing with a simple bow.

PEACHY SHELL

Honesty (silver dollar)
Soft pink helichrysum (strawflowers)
Small white helichrysum (strawflowers)
Pink hare's tail grass
Large shell
Florists' dry foam
Stub wire

The colours of this pretty conch shell have been cleverly picked out in the soft pinks and creams of the delicate arrangement.

First wedge some foam into the neck of the shell. Then wire up a few honesty seed-heads and push them into the foam. Add some large, pink helichrysum (strawflowers) and fill in the gaps with bunches of small, white helichrysum.

Finally, wire together small bunches of hare's tail grass and dot them among the arrangement so that they stand up above the other flowers, softening the outline.

LEFT: *Little can beat a simple sheaf of scented lavender tied with a natural-style bow.*

Pink peonies, open and in bud
White and pink larkspur
Pink helichrysum (strawflowers)
Pink broom blooms
Willow and myrtle
Shallow basket
Florists' dry foam and adhesive tape
Fast drying clear glue and stub wire
2 plastic pinholders
Fixative

This wall display looks stunning arranged in a shallow basket.

Thread wire through the top of the basket to make a hanger. Using green fixative, secure the plastic pinholders to one side of the base of the basket. Next, place foam on to the pinholders and secure them with adhesive tape. Following the line of the basket, insert the larkspur stems into the foam. Wire the other flowers into short bunches and fill in the display.

Position the peonies to form a central focal line and, to finish, place the helichrysum (strawflowers) below the peonies to create harmony and depth.

ABOVE: Together in this traditional basket, lavender and roses echo the days of Victorian flower sellers.

BELOW: Cream and pink tones combine prettily in this peachy conch shell.

ROSE AND LAVENDER BASKET

Sea lavender
Lavender
Roses
Basket with handle
Reel wire
Satin ribbon
Florists' dry foam

The beauty of this design is that it can be made to any scale — from a large shopping basket to a miniature decorative one.

Start by packing the basket with florists' foam and covering it with sea lavender. Next, wire together bunches of lavender and push these in amongst the sea lavender. Intersperse the display with pretty peach or champagne coloured roses.

Complete the arrangement with some satin ribbon bows, wired on to the base of the basket handle.

BELOW: A swathe of dried flowers in pretty shades of pink works well as a wall hanging when set to one side of a shallow basket.

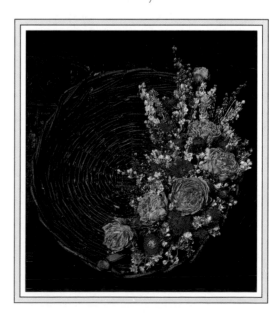

DELPHINIUM DELIGHT

Delphiniums
Pink peonies
Eucalyptus stems
Glass vase
Wire mesh
Florists' adhesive tape

A traditional V-shaped vase is the inspiration for this charming arrangement. The flowers follow the line of the vase, falling into a graceful shape.

First, cut a piece of wire mesh to fit over the top of the vase and secure this in place discreetly with adhesive tape. Carefully position the delphiniums to follow their natural shape and fill in the arrangement with soft sprays of eucalyptus.

Keep the peony stems much shorter and position the flowers to give depth. Finally, arrange a short stem of eucalyptus to drape over the front of the vase.

FLORAL GIFT BOX

Pink peonies
Cream coloured helichrysum (strawflowers)
Spear-shaped eucalyptus (snow gum) leaves
Round gift box
Hot glue gun or all-purpose glue
Stub wire
Lace ribbon

Use hops and lady's mantle for garlanding and softening an otherwise plain household object, like this mirror.

This pretty gift box can be given as a present in its own right. But it's most welcome when filled with another gift, such as potpourri, an attractive scarf or some jewellery set in shredded tissue paper. (See page 146 for more gift box ideas.)

Form a length of lace ribbon into generous loops, securing it with some wire. Make another two or three ribbon loops, then glue them to the top of the box.

Now glue on three or four peonies to the centre of the box. Among them tuck in a few leaves and helichrysum (strawflowers). Finally, work out toward the edge of the box with more helichrysum and the spear-shaped eucalyptus leaves.

LEFT: Lacy peonies and creamy helichrysum nestle amongst lace gathers on this simple Floral Gift Box.

FAR LEFT: The strong contours of deep purple delphiniums and pale pink peonies form an attractive display.

HOP AND ROSE MIRROR

Hops
Lady's mantle
Poppy seedheads
Deep red roses
Wicker framed mirror
All-purpose glue

This attractive natural mirror can be treated rather like a traditional vine wreath, with flowers and leaves slotting into the circle to form a decorative ring.

There are always irregularities on a ring such as this and you can ease the twisted wicker slightly with the points of a pair of scissors, so that the plant material can be pushed in between. It is also a good idea to use dabs of all-purpose glue to secure those pieces which are too delicate to push into the frame.

Arrange the lady's mantle first, inserting small clusters at intervals all around the frame. Then add clumps of hops and a few poppy seedheads. Put more clusters — particularly of bushy hops — at the top of the frame. Finish with a cluster of rich, red roses and their leaves. These flowers are best attached to the top of the frame with glue, as their stems will break if pushed too hard into the wicker.

HELICHRYSUM IN STONEWARE

Helichrysum (strawflowers)
Florists' dry foam
Old stoneware kitchen jars

Although quite an extravagant arrangement, these stunning helichrysum in bold reds, magentas and creamy yellows, will last for well over a year before fading.

To make one jarful of the flowers shown here, you will need almost 200 flowers. Of course, you can scale down the whole display and make a smaller arrangement in a smaller jar if you prefer.

If you are drying the helichrysum yourself, they will need their stems wired before they are dried. This is explained on page 39. You will find that most bought helichrysum are wired ready for use.

Pack the jar with foam and begin with a flower in the centre. As a guide, it should be slightly taller than the height of the jar. Now insert more helichrysum to form a dome shaped outline, letting ones toward the rim of the jar drape over the edge. The easiest way to achieve an even outline is to keep turning the jar and inserting the flowers at intervals until you have established a strong shape. You can then fill in the gaps with more helichrysum.

Jars of glowing helichrysum (strawflowers)
make a bold mantelpiece decoration that
will last for many months.

ABOVE: Vibrant yellow flowers set into this little pomander bring a touch of sunshine into the bedroom.

makes a delightfully natural decoration to hang on your door. The added bonus is that this combination of flowers and cones is remarkably inexpensive to assemble.

Wire together clumps of sea lavender and virtually cover the entire moss wreath with it. Next, take some purple statice and wire together several bunches. Intersperse the purple statice evenly amongst the sea lavender and then, at regular intervals, insert some wired clumps of yarrow and sunray. Gather about 10-12 large cones and wire them together in a large bunch. With more wire fix the cones to the base of the wreath. Pull a few strands of flowers between the cones to help offset them.

To finish, intersperse a few more of the cones throughout the wreath to add an interesting contrast of tone and texture to your winter arrangement.

GOLDEN POMANDER

Small yellow helichrysum (strawflowers)
Florists' dry foam sphere
Ribbon
Stub wire

You can hang this pretty pomander from a dressing table or wardrobe door for a feminine touch to a bedroom.

First, make a loop from the ribbon and wire it into the sphere, pushing the wire right through to the base. Trim the wire and then bend the end back into the foam.

Next, insert the helichrysum, packing the flowers tightly into the ball and keeping them all at the same height to maintain the round shape.

Finish with a double bow, wiring it into the top of the pomander.

A WINTER'S WREATH

Sea lavender
Purple statice
Yarrow
Tiny clustered sunray (Helipterum)
Cones
Moss wreath
Stub wire

This attractive winter's wreath in muted creams and golds with a dash of purple

BELOW: Clusters of gold and cream flowers form the basis of this lovely Winter's Wreath.

Herbs and flowers make an attractive decoration for a front door or pretty window.

HANGING BUNCH

*Lavender
Southernwood
Rosemary
Ornamental onion
Cinnamon sticks
Sea lavender
Reel wire
Raffia*

Small bunches of herbs and flowers were once used to repel insects and moths. Today, such bunches have lost none of their properties and they look decorative too. Lavender can also be used on its own, bunched into a 'bottle' (see page 145).

Gather the herbs, ornamental onion and sea lavender into an attractive bunch and wire the stems together securely. Next, wire together two or three cinnamon sticks and bind these on to the bunch, aligning them with the stems. Wire more cinnamon sticks together and set these across the first bunch. Finally, cover any visible wires with raffia strands and finish off with a raffia loop to hang the bunch up.

SILVER POSY

*Lily of the valley
Grape hyacinths
Cornflowers
Pansies
Astrantia
Narcissi
Pulmonaria
Spurge
Salad burnet (garden burnet) leaves
Silver bowl
Florists' stub wire
Wire mesh*

All the flowers in this pretty miniature display have been carefully preserved in silica gel (see page 37 for details). This method of preservation retains the colour and form of the flowers well, and for more delicate specimens, such as narcissi, it is the only preservation method suitable.

Once preserved, it is best to strengthen the delicate stems by wiring them.

Fill the bowl with crushed wire mesh and gently insert the wired flowers to build up a triangular shape. Use the pansies as the focal flowers. Dried foliage can be added to hide any visible wires.

LILAC NET

*Red amaranthus (love-lies-bleeding)
Blue larkspur
Soft pink, cluster-flowered
helichrysum (strawflowers)
Basket with handle
Pot-pourri (for recipes, see pages 87-97)
Lilac coloured netting
Stub wire*

Soft net has been used here to create a soft, billowing effect.

Wire together clumps of amaranthus and insert them at intervals around the rim of the basket. Angle them for more interest.

Fill in the display with clusters of larkspur and helichrysum sprays, forming a dense ring of flowers around the basket. Now tie bows of lilac net to the basket handle and fill the bowl with pot-pourri.

RIGHT: It is difficult to believe that all the flowers in this pretty Silver Posy are preserved and not fresh.

BELOW: Lilac net brings out the blues and purples of this lovely pot-pourri basket.

ABOVE: This decorative nosegay also has the practical purpose of repelling moths.

MOTH REPELLENT NOSEGAY

Dried lavender
Lavender bottles (see page 145)
Roses
Southernwood
Nipplewort
Wire
Velvet ribbon

Dried flowers and herbs have been used for centuries to keep harmful insects away from susceptible fabrics. This particular design is ideal for keeping moths at bay, and is pretty enough to use as a decoration in its own right, hung on the back of a bedroom door, for example.

To make the bunch, simply bind all the flowers together with wire. Tie some velvet ribbon around the stems and form it into a loop for hanging the nosegay.

As well as lavender and southernwood, other plants you could use for repelling moths include sea lavender, lady's mantle and sprigs of rosemary. Roses and other pretty flowers can also be added for decorative purposes.

COFFEE SACKS

Yellow and beige sea lavender
Wild oats
Phalaris
Wheat
Ornamental onion
Bells of Ireland
Brown plants such as Ti-tree,
Leptocarpus, Gynerium, Carex pendula
Rust coloured eucalyptus
Teasels
Safflowers
Sorrel
Sunray (Helipterum)
Yarrow
Tiny cones
Small coffee sacks
Florists' dry foam
Crumpled newspaper or tissue paper

The rough hessian of coffee sacks provides a good backdrop for these natural displays. You can experiment with any number of

reeds, dried grasses and cereal plants in their natural colours. Any other brown, beige or rust coloured plants will also complement well. Touches of colour here and there to lift the displays are provided by the orange tips of the safflowers and the cheerful white heads of the sunrays.

Push a brick of florists' foam into the sack and pack the sack out with tissue paper or crumpled newspaper.

In one sack, form a softly curving outline with the grasses, wired cones and foliage,

until you have a dense display. Fill in the centre with the safflowers and yarrow.

The second sack achieves a different effect using beige sea lavender, a sweeping spray of teasels and some striking white sunrays. Follow the lines shown here to create a well-balanced arrangement.

BELOW: A medley of grasses, seedheads and cereals in plain coffee sacks echo the simple beauty of the hedgerow.

ABOVE: This straw hat makes a pretty, decorative feature when adorned with sprays of wheat and dahlias.

EDWARDIAN HAT

Orange dahlias
Helichrysum (strawflowers)
Golden rod
Wheat
Dryandra
Quaking grass
Oak foliage
Straw hat
Moss
Reel and stub wire
All-purpose glue and wreath wrap

Try livening up a plain straw boater with this striking floral spray.

Mould the moss into an egg shape and bind it with reel wire. Cover the shape with wreath wrap and secure it to the hat, again with reel wire threaded through the weave.

Cut the wheat stems and save the stalks. Wire the ears into clumps and push them into the moss. Wire in dahlias, helichrysum and oak leaves. Bunch the discarded wheat stems and wire these into one end. Finally, glue leaves around one side of the brim.

FLOWER TREE

*Orange and yellow
helichrysum (strawflowers)
Blue larkspur
Green amaranthus (love-lies-bleeding)
Plastic pot for base
Plaster of Paris
Interesting short, thick branch or
branches for the trunk
Wire mesh
Dry sphagnum moss
Twigs
U-pins
Raffia
Florists' dry foam sphere
Stub wire
Bun moss*

This ever-popular form of floral arrangement is easier to achieve than it looks.

Mix the plaster of Paris with water and pour it into the plastic container. Quickly insert the branch, which will act as the tree trunk, and hold it in position until the plaster has set sufficiently. Leave the plaster to dry for several hours.

Next, form a ring of wire mesh, slightly deeper than the container and wide enough to fit snugly around it. The ring must be double thickness so you can pack it tightly with the dry sphagnum moss. When it is fully packed, neatly bend the raw edges of wire over to close the ring.

Cut the twigs into equal lengths, the depth of the moss ring, and attach them with two U-pins per twig. Cover the pins with two lengths of raffia.

Place the container with the tree trunk inside the wire surround. Take the foam sphere and scrape out a hole for the trunk. Push the sphere down hard on to the trunk, making sure it is held firm.

Decorate the tree by wiring the helichrysum into small bunches and inserting them evenly around the sphere. Keep the tree

LEFT: Don't be daunted – this stunning and colourful flower tree is quite straightforward to assemble.

ABOVE: Rich rusty coloured roses and creamy sunray spill out of a jet black wooden box.

turning to create a round shape. Next, add the larkspur and the amaranthus, tucking them in to retain a neat, spherical shape.

Finish off with a few pieces of bun moss around the base of the tree to hide the plaster and the wire mesh.

LAVENDER WALL DISPLAY

Canary grass
Lavender
Flat-backed wall basket
Florists' dry foam
Plastic coated florists' wire
Knife
All-purpose glue or hot glue gun

Inspired by Elizabethan garden engravings, this attractive wall design is built up by arranging alternate rows of lavender and canary grass.

Fill the wall basket with the florists' dry foam, then trim the foam into a convex shape with a knife.

Cut the canary grass stems to approximately 1in (2.5cm) and insert them around the bottom edge of the basket. Next insert

RIGHT: Rows of canary grass and lavender create a striking wall display.

four rows of lavender and, keeping to the shape of the basket, add another row of canary grass. Work another few rows of lavender, one of canary grass and finish with more lavender.

For a final decorative touch, you can wire together a few stems of the lavender and canary grass into a small bunch and glue it to the front of the basket.

LATE SUMMER ROSES

Bupleurum
Cream sunray (Helipterum)
Rust coloured roses
Black, wooden box
Florists' dry foam

A jet black wooden box provides a frame for this pretty arrangement and helps to bring out the subtle warmth of the roses.

First, cut the florists' foam to fit snugly inside the box. Insert clumps of bupleurum to form the outline and help prop open the lid of the box. Use shorter stems at the front so that they slightly overhang the edge of the box. Fill in the outline with the cream coloured sunray.

Complete the picture with the roses. First, gently steam some of them. This will soften the petals a little so that you can then pull back the outer ones to open out the flowers before you position them.

For the best effect, recess some of the roses deep into the display, keeping one or two more prominent.

RUSTIC BASKET

Peonies
Globe artichoke heads
Deep pink helichrysum (strawflowers)
Poppy seedheads
Sunray (Helipterum)
Pink larkspur
Oats
Quaking grass
Fern leaves
Silver brunia
Basket
Florists' dry foam
Florists' adhesive tape

The freshly gathered look of this display is achieved by carefully selecting flowers and foliage that give an interesting outline and texture to the design.

First, wedge the foam into the centre of the basket. Cut the ferns into 3in (7.5cm) lengths and insert them around the outside edge of the foam to create a 'collar'.

Place a peony in the middle of the foam, just under the basket handle. Cut short bunches of smaller flowers and foliage and wire them into groups. Turning the basket

LEFT: A traditional rustic basket is crammed with delightful garden flowers.

as you work, insert these around the edge.

Finally, build up the centre with poppy seedheads, artichokes and bunches of, as well as individual, flowers.

CHANTILLY LACE

Sea lavender
Love-in-a-mist
Pink larkspur
Lady's mantle
Pink roses
Wicker basket with handle
Wire mesh
Stub wire

Bring a touch of the countryside into your living room with this beautiful arrangement of garden flowers.

First, lay the wire mesh across the top of the basket and secure it to the edges with pieces of stub wire.

Next create a base for the arrangement by packing the basket out with sea lavender. Wire clumps of love-in-a-mist together and insert them throughout the display. Do the same with the lady's mantle. Then add

BELOW: The choice of colours and textures used here are reminiscent of chantilly lace.

ABOVE: A contemporary Autumn Garland made from clusters of nuts, flowers, sponge mushrooms, leaves and seedheads makes a striking feature.

bunches of larkspur to soften the whole effect. Try to avoid obscuring the handle totally with the flowers. Complete the picture with several garden roses.

AUTUMN GARLAND

Oak leaves
Sponge mushrooms
Large and small lotus seedheads
Walnuts
Witch hazel twigs
Yarrow
Twig or vine wreath
Stub wire

This unusual, imaginative wreath makes a striking autumn decoration.

Begin by wiring together small bunches of the oak leaves. Then take a few pieces of dry sponge mushroom and push stub wire through one side of it. Attach the leaves and fungus to the wreath and form three groups, making sure that they are evenly spaced around the ring.

Next, wire up some lotus seedheads and insert these among the other plants. Push a piece of wire into each walnut and twist several together to make small groups. Add these to the display.

Now add a few witch hazel twigs, and finish off with little clumps of yarrow, which provide a welcome splash of colour.

NUT AND CONE ROPE

Cones
Walnuts
Chinese lanterns
Quaking grass
Stub wire
Wide gold giftwrap ribbon

The framework of this seasonal garland is made of cones and walnuts. Wire each cone by wrapping a stub wire around its base. For each walnut, push a stub wire through one end as far as it will go.

Take a group of nuts and cones and twist the wires together. Add to the base of the group with more cones and nuts, twisting the wires together to secure each group. Continue adding cones and nuts in this way until the 'rope' is long enough.

Using the giftwrap ribbon, make a double bow for the top of the rope, adding some additional tails for fullness. Wire this into the display.

Just behind the bow, wire in a long length of ribbon and twist this in and out of the rope until you reach the end; leave a long tail trailing. Cut a swallowtail into the end of the ribbon for a neat finish.

Finally, wire together small groups of Chinese lanterns and quaking grass and intersperse these amongst the cones, entangling the wires to secure them.

LIGHTS AND STARS

Reddish-bronze hydrangeas
Poppy seedheads
Globe artichokes (optional)
Shallow basket with handle
Bronze or copper jug
Silver spray paint
Florists' dry foam
Gold cord
Silver glitter stars

Silver and gold look rich and festive and, mixed with the subtle colours of dried hydrangea flowerheads, they make a luxurious Christmas arrangement. First, spray the hydrangea heads lightly with silver

paint, just enough to frost them without obscuring their natural colour. They will not take long to dry.

In the meantime, wedge a block of florists' dry foam into the basket. Push the silvery hydrangeas into the basket and fill in any gaps with poppy seedheads and add a spiky artichoke head or two if you wish. Tie a gold cord bow on to the handle of the basket for the finishing touch.

For the jug, you will need no mechanics. Simply fill it with silvery hydrangeas and

ABOVE: This attractive Nut and Cone Rope, with its swirling gold ribbon, makes an ideal Christmas decoration. Change the ribbon for a year-round hanging display.

ABOVE: *Use lengths of wide tartan ribbon, tied into generous bows, to create this charming Scottish garland. Clusters of red roses and cream pearl everlasting pick out the colours in the tartan.*

ABOVE: *Dried hydrangea heads, lightly high-lighted with silver, form the basis of this sumptuous Christmas arrangement.*

add some silver glitter stars. (These can be bought, or you could make your own from metallic cardboard, glitter and wire).

Offset the whole display with a shallow dish of floating candles wrapped in gold filigree ribbon, a selection of shiny baubles and some burnished trinket boxes.

SCOTTISH SALUTE

Red roses
Pearl everlasting (Anaphalis)
Twig ring
Stub wire
Wide tartan ribbon

A slightly different festive garland, this design makes the perfect accompaniment to a tartan-trimmed Christmas tree. Wire the roses individually and set them in three small groups into the ring. Now wire together nine small bunches of pearl ever-lasting and push them into the ring so that they surround the roses.

Complete the garland with the ribbon. Tie three lengths into generous single bows and wire them into the three spaces on the ring. For the ribbon tails, cut one more length of ribbon, fold it in half and push a piece of wire through the folded end. Trim the two ends into swallowtails and wire this beneath one of the bows.

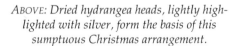

$\mathcal{F}$LOWERS FOR THE TABLE

*A mound of rosy apricots scattered with
cream coloured freesias creates an
eye-catching table decoration.*

*Every table needs a focal point and what better
choice than a selection of beautiful flowers,
whether fresh, dried or even artificial? Add fruit,
candles, ribbon, cones or leaves and turn almost
any container into an exquisite centrepiece.*

*I*n this chapter we have also given you a selection of place settings and napkin ideas so you can make the very best of your table setting — whatever the event.

APRICOTS AND CREAM

Fresh apricots
Ivy leaves
Cream coloured freesias
Narcissi flowerheads
Glass or china cake stand
White paper doily

Mix fruit with flowers and leaves to create this luscious table centrepiece.

To give the leaves a lovely sheen, wash them first and wipe their surface with cooking oil. Then place the white doily on the cake stand and carefully push the ivy leaves underneath it, around the edges.

Arrange the apricots in a pile on the doily. (If they are to be eaten, don't let them touch the ivy which is poisonous, and wash them thoroughly before eating.) Arrange a few sprays of cream coloured freesias around the apricots, slotting in the narcissi, or any other small flowers, between the fruit.

TEA-TIME TREAT

White ranunculus
Sprays of Queen Anne's lace (or any other umbrella-like flowerheads)
Ivy leaves
Green glass sundae dish
Florists' wire mesh coated in green plastic
Florists' tape

In their early stages of flowering, white ranunculus have a greenish tinge which combines beautifully with the sprays of Queen Anne's lace and ivy, to make this charming display. It's a welcome addition to a coffee morning or afternoon tea table.

Secure the crushed mesh into the glass dish with florists' tape. Cut one ranunculus stem to two and a half times the height of the dish and position it in the centre of the display. Surround the central stem with the other ranunculus so that they cascade down and over the edge of the dish.

Finally, add some ivy leaves, and fill any gaps with the Queen Anne's lace and any remaining ranunculus buds.

BELOW: Cascading white ranunculus delight an afternoon tea-tray.

ABOVE: Brighten up plain napkin rings with posies of dried flowers, coral and fine net or a selection of miniature flower clusters.

DINNER TIME DELIGHTS

Tiny dried flowers such as helichrysum (strawflowers), glixia (grass daisies), sunray (Helipterum), and mini poppy seedheads
Larger dried helichrysum flowers
Beard grass (Polypogon)
Coral
Pink spotted netting
Silver florists' wire
Plain wooden or plastic napkin rings
All-purpose glue
White cord

Try decorating some plain napkin rings with a few dried flowers. You can either cover the rings entirely or make a pretty posy to tie on top.

To cover the ring, spread the surface with glue and stick on masses of tiny flowers until it is completely covered.

For the posy, gather a small square of netting in the middle with a long piece of reel wire. Using the same wire, secure strands of beard grass (*Polypogon*) on to the back of the netting. Next, add two pieces of coral, wiring them on in the same way. Finish off by arranging small cluster-flowered sunray flowers over the wire to the front of the netting and then adding three larger helichrysum (strawflowers) on top.

Tie the posy to the napkin ring with a length of white cord. In this way, by simply untying the cord, each of your supper guests can take home a small memento.

YELLOW MELON

Daffodils
Purple hyacinths
Jonquil
Three double white tulips
Stems of eucalyptus
Honeydew melon
Florists' foam

Fruit and flowers make great companions for any buffet or dinner table. Here, a golden honeydew melon makes a practical and pretty container for the flowers.

First, cut a wedge from the melon and scoop out most of the flesh, putting it into the refrigerator to eat later. Then push a piece of soaked florists' foam into the fruit and insert stems of eucalyptus to create an asymmetrical outline.

Now you can arrange the flowers. Begin by cutting the daffodil stems on a slant to make them easier to insert into the foam. Cut one daffodil shorter than the rest and put it in the foreground as the focal flower. Position the other daffodils at increasing heights on one side of the display.

Insert the jonquil to the other side. Bring some through the front of the display and place a couple behind the focal daffodil. Add the hyacinths next and complete the display with the white tulips.

YELLOW ROSE BOWL

Yellow roses
Yellow freesias
Cream spider chrysanthemums
Leucodendron foliage
Silver rose bowl
Wire mesh (if necessary)

Little can beat a traditional rose arrangement set in a silver bowl in the centre of a highly polished dining table.

A traditional rose bowl should have a wire mesh centre to support the blooms; if not, crush some wire mesh and push this into the bowl.

Fill the bowl with water and pack it with the chrysanthemums, cutting the stems short to give a dense base for the other flowers. Then, place the roses in between the chrysanthemums, keeping the stems a little longer. Next, intersperse the arrangement with a few freesias.

Finally, add the *Leucodendron* foliage and freesia buds, ensuring that the stems are slightly longer than those of the other flowers. A full-blown rose at the foot of the bowl will complete the arrangement and last for the duration of the dinner party.

BELOW: Large fruits, such as this melon, make ideal containers for flowers.

ABOVE: Rose bowls are designed to show roses off to their best advantage, as this charming yellow arrangement demonstrates.

LEMON PYRAMID

Lemon roses
Yellow lilies and buds
White stock
Plate
Florists' foam cone

This stunning display makes a wonderful accompaniment to a wedding buffet table or special occasion party. It is also conveniently quick to assemble.

Soak the florists' foam well and stand it on the plate. It should be heavy enough not to need fixing.

Begin with the lilies. Snip out their pollen-laden stamens, which severely stain when brushed against furniture or clothing. Cut their stalks down to about 2in (5cm) and insert the first one into the top of the cone. Work down the sides of the cone, angling each flowerhead slightly for interest. Now add the roses, spacing them out evenly between the lilies. Finally, fill in with short stems of sweet smelling stock.

RIGHT: Pyramid arrangements, such as this Lemon Pyramid, are perfect for buffet tables as they can be clearly seen above the food.

SPRINGTIME BUFFET

Pink hyacinths
White daffodils
Grape hyacinths (Muscari)
Serving dish or cake stand
Wire mesh
Florists' foam cone
Water resistant tape

This elegant serving dish is perfect for a pyramid flower design and makes a superb decoration for a buffet table.

Wrap the foam cone in wire mesh and attach the cone to the dish with the tape. Now soak the cone well with water.

Insert a hyacinth bud at the top of the cone and, turning the dish around, add the remaining hyacinths, graduating in size down toward the edge of the dish to create the pyramid shape.

Tuck in white daffodils between the sprays of hyacinths and finally add the rich blue grape hyacinths to define the shape and provide colour contrast.

ABOVE: The subtle colours and low-lying arrangement make Harmony an elegant and stylish dinner party centrepiece.

ABOVE: Dark green ivy provides the foil for the candles and cream freesias in this stylish centrepiece.

LEFT: A collection of hyacinths and daffodils, this delightful springtime arrangement will enhance any special occasion buffet table.

IVY CANDLE RING

White freesias
Trailing ivy stems
Circular cake base
Drawing pins
Modelling clay or florists' putty
Selection of white and green candles

This attractive candle ring, with its elegant dark green and white colour scheme, will suit any special occasion. Make this display on the evening of the event as the ivy withers if kept too long. In order to keep the freesias fresh you can bind the stem ends with a little wet cotton wool.

Begin by attaching strands of ivy to the edge of the cake base with drawing pins. Build up the ring by adding more strands and bunches of leaves until only a small space remains in the centre. Insert stems of freesia among the ivy leaves to provide colour contrast. Push blobs of modelling clay or florists' putty into the centre of the display and insert a mixture of white and green candles of varying heights.

HARMONY

Mauve freesias
Mauve roses
Mauve sweet peas
Purple anemones
Ivy
Eucalyptus foliage
Silver dish
Glass bowl
Florists' foam and tape

The beautiful floral fretwork on the silver dish used for this arrangement looks stunning against the dark wood of the dining table and harmonizes well with the mauve and purple blooms.

Place a glass bowl filled with foam inside your silver dish and secure the foam with florists' tape. Soak the foam well with water. Place stems of the different leaves around the edge of the dish, allowing the ivy to trail on to the table.

Insert a rose in the centre of the bowl and position the remaining roses to graduate down to the rim of the dish. Add the sweet peas, freesias and dark anemones among the roses, letting these, like the ivy, also trail on to the table. Finish off with an occasional ivy leaf peeping through the flowers to add to the display.

FLORAL PLACECARD

Small bunch of dried lavender
Flower picture from Victorian découpage
scraps, a greeting card or magazine
Glue stick
Thin white cardboard
Scissors
Coloured paper
Narrow mauve ribbon or fine cord

This novel idea for a place setting looks particularly pretty on floral china.

Roughly cut out the flower picture and stick it on to some thin white cardboard for support. Now carefully cut around the edges of the flowers leaving a ½in (lcm) strip of card at the bottom. Fold this strip forward — as well as bearing the guest's name, you will find that it also helps the placecard to stand up.

On the coloured paper, write the name of your guest, cut this out and stick it on to the folded strip, trimming it as necessary. To support the card, glue a triangle of cardboard at right angles on to the back of the card to act as a stand.

Finally, tie the lavender together with the narrow cord or ribbon and set it to the side of the placecard.

You can, of course, use any small dried flowers for this design. Try picking out a principal colour from your chosen flower picture. Or you could even coordinate the design with your table linen or crockery.

BELOW: A little bunch of dried lavender sets off this hand-made placecard beautifully.

VIOLET POSY

Bunch of violets
White lace napkin
Narrow lilac and white ribbon

Perfect for a side plate, your guests can take these miniature posies home with them. Do not be tempted to put these out until your guests assemble, as you will find that the violets wither quickly.

ABOVE: Tiny flowers, such as these pretty violets, make exquisite posies for side plates.

Tie small bunches of violets together with narrow lilac and white ribbon and set them to the side of a pretty linen or lacy napkin. You can echo the posies by clustering bunches of violets together in shallow dishes in the table centre and by trailing wider ribbon across the table.

ANEMONE TRIM

Fresh anemone or similar flower
Plain napkin
Florists' medium gauge wire
Florists' silver reel wire
A few little silk or paper flowers
Narrow ribbon
All-purpose glue

This charming flower-trimmed napkin ring adds a touch of elegance to a table setting and is very easy to make.

Bend a short length of medium gauge wire into a circle; twist the ends together to secure them. Wind the fine wire around the silk or paper flowers to form a bunch, then twist the ends around the wire circle to hold the flowers in place.

Disguise the wire circle by covering it with the narrow ribbon. Hold one end of the ribbon in place with one hand, and use the other hand to twist the ribbon around the circle to cover it completely, beginning and ending underneath the flowers. Secure the ends with glue.

Insert the napkin and, for the finishing touch, tuck in a fresh bloom: anemones are a good choice. As the fresh flower will not last long, add it just before your guests sit down for dinner.

BELOW: Mix fresh and artificial flowers for this attractive Anemone Trim napkin ring.

FLOATING ANEMONES

Anemones
Laurustinus flowers
Gypsophila (baby's breath)
Large and small glass bowls
Marbles (optional)

This arrangement makes an ideal centrepiece for any table but especially a low coffee table.

First, fill the larger bowl with water, then take 12-15 anemones and cut their stems down to around 1in (2.5cm). Float the flowers in the water, filling in any gaps with sprigs of laurustinus.

ABOVE: Anemones make superb floating flowers. Try this display at a buffet where guests can view the flowers from above.

You will find that an occasional pale pink or white anemone lifts the solid mass of colour, so don't use only dark flowers.

The smaller bowl is a perfect complement to the larger one. For added effect, put a handful of glass marbles into the bowl before adding the water. Float a few anemone heads on the water, adding a sprig or two of gypsophila to break up the density. Allow some of the marbles to be seen through the flowerheads.

FRUIT AND IVY

Ivy
Apples
Grapes
Chincherinchee flowers
Plastic plate
Florists' foam and glue
Three candle holders
Three candles of different heights
Wire U-pins
Cocktail sticks

This elegant centrepiece is quickly assembled and lasts well. It's particularly suitable in the winter months when fresh flowers are in short supply.

Glue a block of florists' foam to the centre of the plate and, when bonded, trim away the upper edges of the foam diagonally. Dampen the foam well and add the three candle holders to the centre. Push the candles into the holders.

Now hide the candle holders with short stems of trailing ivy and push larger leaves into the foam to cover the plate. Push the apples on to cocktail sticks and insert them at random into the foam. (Angle them dif-

BELOW: Glossy green ivy acts as a foil to the paler greens of the apples and grapes in this exotic centrepiece.

ferently to give more interest.) Next add small bunches of grapes into the display, securing them with the U-pins.

Fill in any gaps with chincherinchee flowerheads and individual grapes pushed on to cocktail sticks.

If you plan to eat the fruit, you must wash it after removing it from the display — contact of the fruit with the poisonous ivy could make you ill. Alternatively, use vine leaves as a base for the fruit.

HEAVENLY TWINS

Pale pink roses
Clematis and astrantia
Honeysuckle
Green grasses
Variegated mint leaves
Pink peonies
Garden pinks (Dianthus x allwoodii)
Nepeta
Larkspur

Two narrow-stemmed glass vases
Two blocks of florists' foam
Florists' tape and wire netting

A warm summer evening and a candlelit dinner provide the perfect setting for these romantic twin bouquets. The mood is feminine and pretty, with a soft colour scheme of pink and green set off by sparkling glass and lace. Although twins, these displays should not be identical.

Cut pieces of soaked foam to fit into each vase and trim the tops to about 2in (5cm) above the rim. Cover the foam with wire netting, taping it to the rim of the vase with florists' tape.

The grasses and longest flowers, such as the nepeta, clematis, pinks and honeysuckle,

---

BELOW: Roses and honeysuckle add a delicious fragrance to these elegant twin arrangements.

ABOVE: Candles add sparkle to any party and combined with scented rose petals make spectacular table centrepieces.

---

are inserted first to create a triangular outline. Now add some shorter stems, inserting more grasses at the front to sweep out and down over the front of the pedestal. Insert the largest blooms into the centre. Finally, fill in any gaps with the remaining richly scented roses, honeysuckle and mint, which give a heady romantic aroma.

CANDLELIT PETALS

Scented rose petals
Aluminium jelly mould
Florists' putty
A selection of thin candles of varying lengths

Scented petals floating in water have been used to decorate this shiny jelly mould and set the scene for tall, thin candles.

Push some florists' putty on to the base of the jelly mould and insert the candles, keeping the lengths varied for interest.

Now top up the mould with water and float handfuls of scented rose petals on the surface to hide the putty.

DANCING LIGHTS

Golden orange chrysanthemum heads
Shallow glass dish
Floating yellow candles

One of the simplest table displays — floating candles and flowerheads — can also be the most effective. The candlelights dance on the water giving a flattering light to any dinner or supper party.

Fill a shallow glass pie or fruit dish with water and add four or five floating candles. Float 12-14 chrysanthemum flowerheads alongside the candles.

Light the candles when you are ready to eat; they last at least four hours.

HARVEST NAPKIN

A few dried stems of canary grass
Stems of wheat
Dried orange statice
Straw placemat
White napkin
1¾ yd (1.5 metres) of beige ribbon
Thread

This simple place setting makes an attractive accompaniment to any Thanksgiving or Harvest supper table.

Cut the ribbon into three equal lengths and tie these together at one end. Plait them until the plait is long enough to tie around the napkin twice with a little left over.

In Dancing Lights, a glass dish gives maximum sparkle to bobbing candles and floating flowerheads.

Next, group the wheat, grasses and statice together and secure them with a piece of thread or fine wire.

Then fold the napkin in half twice to form a long, thin rectangle. Lay the flowers on top of the napkin and wind the plaited ribbon around the napkin and the flowers twice, tying the ends under the napkin.

For added variety, you could match the plaited ribbon to the colour of the statice. For a less autumnal look, use purple or blue statice instead of the orange.

 68

ABOVE: Cake stands make excellent table centrepieces. The brightly coloured flowers used here have been assembled to resemble a rich gateau.

BELOW: Complement a scrubbed pine table and straw placemats with this natural Harvest Napkin tie.

RUSTIC CENTREPIECE

Cones
Walnuts
Preserved oak leaves
Dried winged everlasting or
sandflowers (Ammobium)
Small cork mat or cake base
Small block of dry florists' foam
Florists' wire
Florists' tape
White candle

This woodland design using nuts, cones and leaves makes the perfect centrepiece for a stripped pine or plain wooden table, especially in a country kitchen.

Begin by taping a block of dry florists' foam on to a small cork mat or cake base. Wire up several cones and walnuts, forcing the wire through the base of each nut as far as it will go.

Wire together clumps of oak leaves and build up the outline of the display. Now insert the nuts and cones, placing the walnuts in small clusters. Keep the shape irregular to make it more interesting.

Brighten the display by scattering small clumps of winged everlasting throughout. To finish, trim a candle to the required length and push it firmly into the foam.

FLORAL GATEAU

Yellow roses
Alstroemeria
Leucodendron brunia
Red ranunculus
Mimosa
Coloured glass cake stand
Florists' foam

This sumptious arrangement of plump flowers on a glass cake stand looks almost edible. To make sure that this display lasts, condition the flowers before you arrange them (see pages 148-151 for details).

Soak the piece of florists' foam well and place it in the centre of the stand. Insert the roses and alstroemeria alternately around the edge of the foam; keep the stems short so that when inserted into the foam the flowerheads rest on the edge of the dish.

The next layer is created with bobbly *Leucodendron brunia* flowers. Above this, place your layer of bright red ranunculus. Finally, top the 'gateau' with a few sprays of brilliant yellow mimosa.

BELOW: The warm browns of autumn come together in this lovely Rustic Centrepiece, perfect for a cosy supper party.

CHRISTMAS CANDLES

Preserved ruscus (butcher's broom) leaves
Poppy seedheads sprayed gold
Dried white pearl everlasting (Anaphalis)
Dried red roses
Three red candles
Cork mat or cake base
Three blocks of dry florists' foam
All-purpose glue

Why not add a touch of style to the dinner table this festive season with this striking, long-lasting display?

Take a flat circular base, such as a cork mat or cake base, and glue some single ruscus (butcher's broom) leaves around the edge. Stick the blocks of dry florists' foam on top of the base and trim each one to a slightly different height.

Now insert the red candles into the foam, cutting them down to vary their heights.

Build up the arrangement using the gold-sprayed poppy heads, pearl everlasting and more ruscus leaves. The white adds essential highlights to the arrangement. Finish off by scattering single red roses throughout the display.

The colours chosen here are especially for Christmas, but for other times of the year you can use different colours.

BELOW: Rich red, dark green and gold are the traditional colours of Christmas Candles, a long-lasting table display.

ABOVE: For Christmas Splendour, a sumptuous pyramid of seedheads and dried flowers sits on a base of gold-sprayed netting.

CHRISTMAS SPLENDOUR

Dried Chinese lanterns, sprayed gold
Lotus seedheads, sprayed gold
Dried honesty (silver dollar)
Miniature cluster-flowered
helichrysum (strawflowers)
White leaf skeletons
Rose de tefe
Circular cake base
Netting sprayed gold
Red fabric or wide ribbon
Dry florists' foam cone
All-purpose glue
Florists' wire

This sumptuous decoration is the perfect accompaniment to a Christmas buffet table.

Take the cake base and glue the dry foam cone to the centre. Then glue or staple a length of gold netting around the edge of the base, gathering it into bunches as you go. Cut the fabric or ribbon into several lengths and crumple these into double loops. Wire the ends. Arrange them in a ring on top of the gold net.

Wire the ends of the Chinese lanterns and lotus seedheads and insert them evenly into the cone. Intersperse several rose de tefe throughout, pushing them deep into the arrangement. Add highlights with a few stems of honesty (silver dollar).

Wire together bunches of red helichrysum (strawflowers) and dot them among the other plants to add colour throughout. Finally, insert a few groups of leaf skeletons into the display.

FESTIVE TABLE

Three dried globe artichokes
Dried poppy seedheads
Dried bupleurum
Dried buxifolium (sand myrtle)
Dried miniature helichrysum (strawflowers)
Dried fern leaves
Dried rhododendron leaves
Dried reindeer moss
Several cones of varying size
Three large white candles
Two vine wreaths – 9½in (24cm) and
12in (30cm) in diameter
Plate
Florists' putty, stub wire, reel wire and tape
2yd (2 metres) of red and 1 yd (1 metre) of tartan ribbon
Fire retardant spray

Ideal for gracing a buffet table or sideboard, this splendid Christmas design will last throughout the holiday from Christmas Eve right through to Hogmanay.

Fix the putty to the centre of the plate and press in the candles. Place the large wreath over the plate and build up the foliage and bupleurum at the back, leaning it away from the candles. After this, add some fern around the perimeter.

Insert poppy heads, cones, artichokes and moss into the wreath to one side of the candles. Make bows from the ribbons to fill

the other side. These will also need to be wired before being inserted.

To wire the cones, take a piece of stub wire and wind one end around the cone under the broadest part. The other end of the wire serves as a 'stem'.

Lean the small wreath against the front of the large one, and fill in the centre with the remaining items. Finally, coat the display with fire retardant spray. If the candles burn down quickly, simply replace them. Remember to make sure that none burns within 1in (2.5cm) of the dried ingredients.

The glorious colours of tartan combine with a variety of dried seeds, cones and foliage to provide this enduring Festive Table display.

PRESSED FLOWERS

Pressed flowers made into a simple picture are shown off to perfection in an antique frame.

The art of pressing flowers is yet another absorbing pastime to be enjoyed from growing, gathering and collecting flowers and foliage. By pressing flowers, you will have the perfect medium for creating pictures and patterns of lasting beauty. You can turn them into gifts or treasures for your own home.

 72

There's a multitude of plant material you can press successfully. If you are careful how you press, the colour and form of the original plant can be captured for lasting pleasure.

WHAT TO SELECT

Annuals, perennials, shrubs and trees — whether from the garden, patio or florist — all provide material for pressing. Even if you only have a window box, you can sow alyssum, candytuft, forget-me-nots, lobelia and polyanthus.

There's also a huge range of common wild flowers, leaves and grasses to be gathered on a country walk. But do take care. Don't break off stems or pull up root: cleanly cut the parts you require with scissors. And do pay attention to the official list of protected plants that you may not pick.

It is worth attempting to press almost anything: don't forget tendrils, interesting stems, grasses and seedheads. The only types to avoid are succulent and fleshy flowers as these contain too much moisture to press successfully.

WHEN TO PICK AND PRESS

The best time to pick flowers for pressing is toward midday when all the dew has evaporated. Sunny weather is best and rainy days should be avoided. If you have to pick flowers when the weather is damp, pick whole stems, and stand them indoors in water until the petals are dry. Choose flowers that have just opened and before they have produced pollen, but gather some buds as well.

The same goes for bought flowers. Don't be tempted to enjoy them first, but press them when they are at their best. You also need to be aware of varying sizes, unusual shapes, a variety of tints and veining and interesting visual textures, as these are the elements that will not be lost in preserving.

Remember as you are pressing that you can thin out collective flowerheads such as candytuft, wild parsley and hydrangea, so don't pass over large-headed flowers in the belief that they won't press well. Multi-petalled or thick-centred flowers, such as roses, carnations and marguerites, will also need to be broken down into separate parts for pressing. Their parts can be used individually or they can be reassembled to their more familiar form.

BELOW: Small flowers, such as primroses and forget-me-nots, are ideal for pressing. Pick them toward midday on a sunny day.

How to Press Flowers

In most cases, you should sandwich the flowers you want to press between two sheets of absorbent paper — such as blotting paper — and two sheets of stiff cardboard or layers of newspaper. Put the whole 'sandwich' into a flower press or, if you don't have a press, lay it on a flat surface and weigh it down with large books.

If you are using a press, screw the lid down gently to start, then tighten it daily for the first few days, and less frequently thereafter. The plants should take between six to eight weeks to dry; the time required will depend on the varieties used.

When the flowers are ready, lift them off the paper with a palette knife, tweezers or a fine paint brush and store them in a dark place until you wish to use them — glassine photographic bags are ideal for this.

Small flowers and leaves
Small flowers and leaves should be placed face down on some smooth toilet tissue on top of the blotting paper. Use a paint brush to move the pieces into place. Cover them with more tissue before using another sheet of blotting paper and thick cardboard.

Remember, you can press whole sprays as well as individual flowerheads.

Large and multi-petalled flowers
For large flowers, cut away all the harder parts and place the flowers directly on to the blotting paper. Flowers pressed in profile need to be cut in half lengthways.

Multi-petalled flowers such as roses and carnations must be broken down into separate petals before pressing and, depending on their size, should be pressed directly between blotting paper or toilet tissue. Press the stems, sepals and bracts in a press

Fresh flowers may be pressed all through the summer and set aside for use during the winter months.

devoted to thick items. In this press, always use twice as much newspaper as usual between the layers.

Don't forget to use flowers from shrubs and blossom from trees. Cut the backs off trumpet-shaped flowers when pressing flat, but leave the bloom whole when it is being pressed in profile.

Leaves
The best leaves to use are the young ones from cherry, carrot, wild parsley, meadowsweet, rose, silverweed, wild strawberry, vetch, maple, sumach (sumac) and virginia creeper. These press well, as do autumn coloured leaves which have part

74

of their water content removed naturally, due to the season. As with flowers, cut or pull the leaves from the stems and arrange on blotting paper. If they are thick, put them in a press reserved for such material.

BELOW: You can easily make your own flower press using plywood and four sets of nuts and bolts. Add tabs to each layer to help you identify which plants you have pressed and when you pressed them.

MAKING A FLOWER PRESS

Two pieces of ³⁄₈ in (1cm) plywood measuring 10 ³⁄₄ in (27.5cm) square
Clamp
Hand drill
Sandpaper and matt varnish
Four ¹⁄₄ in by 8in (7mm by 20cm) fully threaded bolts with washers and wing nuts
Strong glue
Newspapers
Double-walled corrugated cardboard and blotting paper cut into 9in by 10in (22.5cm by 25.5cm) rectangles.

To make your own flower press, clamp the two pieces of plywood together and drill four ³⁄₁₆in (5mm) holes in each corner, ³⁄₄in (18mm) from the sides. Open up the holes in the top square to ⁵⁄₁₆in (8mm). Sand all the surfaces and apply a coat or two of matt varnish. When the varnish is dry, screw in the bolts, applying a little glue to the bottom threads just before screwing them home to fix them permanently.

Make up layers from the corrugated cardboard, blotting paper and newspaper. Each cardboard 'sandwich' should contain 12 sheets of newspaper with two sheets of blotting paper in the centre.

ABOVE: Small flowers, such as forget-me-nots, should be placed face down on smooth toilet tissue on top of the blotting paper. Cover them with more of the tissue before applying another sheet of blotting paper.

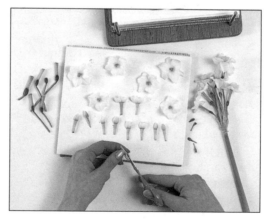

ABOVE: Cut away the hard parts of large flowers, such as narcissi, with sharp scissors. Flowers to be pressed in profile should be cut in half first. For added interest, remember to press some buds as well.

ABOVE: Multi-petalled flowers such as roses and carnations should be carefully broken down into separate petals before pressing. Press stems, sepals and bracts separately in a press devoted to thick items.

in with the remaining pink alyssum, pink verbena, Queen Anne's lace and sorrel.

Clean the picture frame glass carefully, and set it aside in a dust free place for the static electricity to dissipate. Place the glass over the design, and then add the frame. Turn the whole frame over and secure the back, sealing it with tape.

A ROSE REMEMBERED

Rose petals and leaves
Centre from a rock rose
Circular wooden picture frame
Lightweight white cardboard
Pencil and eraser
Scissors
Latex adhesive and tape

Multi-petalled flowers, like roses, are carefully pulled apart before they are pressed. Here, the petals are reassembled into a familiar rose shape.

From the coloured paper, cut a circular mount to fit the frame. Lay the mount over the white cardboard and very lightly pencil in the inside circle of the mount.

Begin the design with individual rose leaves, slightly overlapping each one, and laying them in a circle with the leaf tips

BELOW: Recreate the glory and richness of a deep scarlet rose in this handsome picture.

SILVER LINING

Lady's mantle foliage
Pink alyssum
Pink verbena
Potentillas
Queen Anne's lace (or any
other umbrella-like flowerheads)
Rose and sorrel flowers and foliage
Silver-plated picture frame
Ivory coloured satin
Polyester wadding
Latex adhesive and tape

This type of picture provides a charming way to keep alive the happy memories of flowers received at a special celebration such as a silver wedding anniversary.

ABOVE: Capture the joy of special celebration flowers in a pretty silver frame.

Remove the back from your picture frame, place it on your work surface and cover it with polyester wadding and ivory silk, which you have cut to size.

Using latex adhesive, secure the pressed rose leaves into a triangular shape. Strip the leaves from a few stems and place these stems at the centre of the base to give a bunched effect. Then position the largest potentilla flowers to create a focal point. Highlight the arrangement with the silver underside of lady's mantle leaves.

Finally, soften the effect by positioning sprays of sorrel flowers and foliage and fill

about ⅛ in (3mm) from the pencilled circle. Then secure each of the leaves with a dab of latex adhesive.

Next, select large rose petals and repeat this process, overlapping the top of the petals with the leaves. When the glue has dried, carefully rub out the pencil line and blow away the rubbings.

Now form an inner circle with smaller petals in the same way. Put a dab of glue in the centre of the petals and carefully slide the centre of a rock rose on to the glue.

Once the design is complete, place the mount over the design card, being careful to centre it, and then position the cleaned glass over both.

Carefully transfer them to the frame and secure the back with tape.

VICTORIAN MINIATURE

*Wild rose flowers, buds
and foliage
Forget-me-not flowers and foliage
Small oval picture frame
Polyester wadding
A piece of calico
Latex adhesive and tape*

Wild roses and forget-me-nots mounted in an old-style golden frame echo the design of the pretty Victorian teapot.

First, cut a piece of calico and wadding to fit the frame. Take out the picture back, lay it on your work surface and cover it with the wadding and then the calico. Next, arrange your irregular outline of foliage,

Echoes of a Victorian age: this little pressed flower picture uses only roses and forget-me-nots and their foliage.

broken with sprays of rosebuds. Place a cluster of wild rose flowers in the centre and position some forget-me-nots to highlight the roses.

Apply a small dot of latex adhesive to the centre underside of each flower or leaf, then press the plants down gently, but firmly, into position. Cover the completed design with the cleaned glass, and then add the frame itself.

Finally, pick up the whole frame, carefully turn it over and fix on the back, sealing it securely with tape.

DECORATIVE DOOR PLATES

Selection of pressed flowers and leaves:
those used here are montbretia (Crocosmia),
potentilla, autumn leaves,
narcissus, meadowsweet, buttercup,
cowslip and cornflower
Door plates (from craft suppliers)
Coloured paper
Thin foam rubber
Protective film
Latex adhesive
Marker pen
Hole punch

These specially designed door plates are available from most good craft suppliers. Decorate them with pressed flowers for a highly individual touch that can suit any room in the house.

Cut a piece of coloured paper to fit the recess behind the door plate. Punch corresponding holes in the paper to match those in the door plate, then begin your design.

Once your design is complete, reassemble the door plate by fitting a piece of foam behind the paper and sealing the back with a piece of protective film.

The door plate on the far left uses sprays of montbretia buds (Crocosmia), autumn leaves and potentilla. The centre design has three little vignettes that have been drawn on with a marker pen; the flowers are meadowsweet, buttercup and cowslip. The final door plate has tiny florets of cornflower and narcissus 'Sol d'Or' snaking up it.

AUTUMN LAMPSHADE

Autumnal coloured leaves
Lampshade kit (or re-use an old
lampshade frame)
Lampshade parchment
Latex adhesive
Contact adhesive
Iron-on protective film

The flaming colours of autumn leaves can be captured for their lasting beauty in this handsome lampshade. Alternatively, you could try using pressed flowers for a more

Bring a touch of flair into your home with these stylish and highly individual door plates decorated with pressed flowers.

Autumn sumach (sumac) leaves
Pink larkspur flowers and buds
Rue leaves
Two thick candles
Latex adhesive
Self-adhesive protective film

Pressed-flower designs can transform plain, thick candles, and turn them into attractive decorations. But be careful not to let the candle burn down below the protective film as the designs are not flameproof!

For the yellow candle, fix three autumn sumach leaves in little sprays around the base with latex adhesive.

The other candle is decorated with pink larkspur flowers fixed around the base. Rue leaves are tucked in and around the flowers, and larkspur buds are added a little above the foliage.

To finish, carefully cover both designs with a layer of protective film, allowing an extra $\frac{1}{4}$in (5mm) above the design. Rub the film down carefully and try to avoid trapping any air bubbles.

BELOW: Autumn leaves and larkspur flowers have been used to decorate chunky candles.

summery effect. You can either buy a lampshade kit from a craft shop, or you could carefully dismantle an old lampshade so that you can re-use the frame and use the old material as a pattern.

Cut the parchment to fit the frame of your lampshade. Lay it on your work surface and position the pressed leaves on top in a casual, windswept style. Make sure that you leave about 1in (2.5cm) clear at the top and the bottom of the parchment and that the most interesting leaves are positioned toward the centre of your design.

When you have achieved the desired effect, pick up each leaf in turn and apply a small dot of latex adhesive to the back. Then, carefully placing the leaf back into position, press down on it gently, but firmly, with a clean fingertip for about a minute to ensure that it is secure.

ABOVE: As the light shines through the lampshade, it beautifully illuminates the warm colours of the autumn leaves.

Making sure that there is no dust on the parchment, cover your design with protective film and iron it down according to the manufacturer's instructions. Trim off the surplus film, leaving about $\frac{3}{4}$in (2cm) at one end to overlap.

Run a line of contact adhesive along the top and bottom edges at the levels where the ring of the frame will be. Then run a line of glue along the outside of the lampshade frame rings. When the glue is dry, wrap lampshade parchment around the frame supports: the two lines of adhesive will stick on contact. Iron down the overlapped edge of protective film to finish.

CARNATION COASTERS

Carnation petals in various colours
Cow parsley florets (alternatively, meadow
parsley or wild carrot)
Glass drinks coasters (from craft suppliers)
Green cartridge paper
Scissors
Latex adhesive

Make a set of attractive and practical drinks coasters using pressed carnations in a variety of colours.

Cut a circle of cartridge paper to fit the recess of the coaster. Then form an outer circle of larger carnation petals, fixing them with a little adhesive. Fill in the outer circle with ever decreasing circles of smaller petals. Finish off with a few cow parsley florets for the centre.

Reassemble the coaster, following the manufacturer's instructions.

BELOW: Carnations are pressed petal by petal. Here, they are reassembled to create these lovely drinks coasters.

ENAMEL CANISTER

Mauve candytuft
Salad burnet (garden burnet) leaves
White enamel canister
Adhesive (homecraft) putty or modelling clay
Latex adhesive
Varnish and paintbrush

If you have the patience you can create a whole kitchen range using this simple but pretty pressed-flower design. Canisters like these are inexpensive to buy new or you can pick them up secondhand.

Secure the canister on its side to your work surface with a few blobs of adhesive putty (such as Blu-Tac) to prevent it rolling around while you work.

Take a large head of mauve candytuft and fix it to the centre of the canister with

ABOVE: Decorated white enamelware brightens up any kitchen. You could make a complete range of floral kitchenware this way.

---

latex adhesive. Surround the flower with salad burnet leaves and add two more candytuft flowers on either side.

Protect the design with varnish (either matt polyurethane or the ultra hard 'two pack' type).

For the lid, coat with varnish first before positioning a circle of salad burnet leaves — slightly apart — around the knob. You will find that the tackiness of the varnish sticks the pressed leaves and flowers.

Fill in between the leaves with large, single candytuft petals. When dry, seal the design with two thin coats of varnish, feathering the edges with a lint-free cloth.

LETTER RACK

Lady's mantle leaves
Stems of agrimony
Verbena
Wooden letter rack
Satin varnish and paintbrush

Transform an ordinary wooden letter rack into a handsome wall decoration with the addition of pressed flowers and leaves.

Give the surface to be decorated a coat of satin varnish. Wait for about an hour, until the varnish is partly dry and tacky — it will then be easier to apply the flowers.

Most letter racks have quite narrow slats, so you will need small flowers — we have used flowers with good distinct shapes and strong colours. Position the flowers in an attractive band across each slat and press down firmly against the varnished surface.

When the varnish is completely dry, give the rack one or two more coats.

RIGHT: Pressed flowers are highly suitable for decorating wood. Here they embellish an ordinary letter rack.

PANSY NOTEPAPER

Heart's ease
Maidenhair fern (Venus's hair)
A box of plain notepaper and envelopes
Latex adhesive
Self-adhesive protective film
Matching ribbon

Transform a box of plain stationery into a beautiful gift by adding a few little pressed flowers and fern.

Arrange a small design on the outside flap of the envelopes using just one or two heart's ease and some maidenhair fern. Create a similar design on one corner of most of the sheets of writing paper. (Leave some pieces blank for continuation sheets.) Seal the designs with protective film.

Re-pack the stationery in its box and tie a matching ribbon around the writing paper. For an extra special touch, you can scent the stationery by storing it with pot-pourri before re-packing it.

CRYSTAL MINIATURE

Shepherd's purse
Yellow and pink alyssum
Elderflowers
Heart's ease
Little crystal bowl (from craft suppliers)
Paintbrush
Latex adhesive

This charming miniature design is quite a challenge, but so rewarding when finished.

Remove the white cardboard from the lid of the bowl and use this for your design. Start by forming a crescent outline with tiny pieces of shepherd's purse, using a paintbrush to gently tease the tiny flowers into position. Fill in the outline with florets of the alyssum and elderflower.

Finally, tuck in heart's ease, saving the largest flower for the focal point towards the bottom centre of the crescent shape.

Reassemble the lid following the manufacturer's instructions.

ABOVE: A delicate design using heart's ease, alyssum and elderflower tops a delightful miniature crystal trinket bowl.

SEASONAL CHANGE

Large pansies
Smaller violas
Maidenhair fern (Venus's hair)
Oblong wooden box
Latex adhesive
Iron-on protective film (optional)

The collage of flowers and fern decorating this box can be peeled off and changed at regular intervals to match the season. Or you can seal the design permanently with protective film.

First, place several dots of latex adhesive on the underside of the large pansies and position them on the left-hand side of the box lid. Then take four sprigs of fern and again place dots of adhesive on the underside — position the fern at regular intervals along the box. Next, place a group of violas on the right, and fill in the bottom edge with more fern sprigs.

This design can be made permanent by covering it with a piece of iron-on protec-

LEFT: Create your own scented stationery and decorate it with little pansies and fern.

tive film. Cut an oblong to the exact size of the box top and iron it down with an ordinary domestic iron, making sure you follow the manufacturer's instructions.

WALNUT BOX

Norway maple leaves
Pink larkspur flowers and buds
Water dropwort (or any plant with small,
tightly packed, umbrella-like flowerheads)
Plain wooden box
Matt polyurethane varnish
Paintbrush

Decorate a plain wooden box with pink larkspur and water dropwort and turn it into a treasured casket. Any large leaves make a good backdrop to this design if you have difficulty in obtaining Norway maple.

Give the box a coat of varnish and form an open cluster with the leaves. The varnish will hold the leaves in place.

When the varnish is completely dry, carefully apply a second coat and position a few of the larkspur flowers and buds to one side of the leaf cluster.

On the other side, put a large head of water dropwort or any similar umbrella-like flowerhead. Fill in with some more of the larkspur flowers and individual florets from the water dropwort.

Make sure that the second coat of varnish is dry before finishing off with two more.

BELOW: This pretty flower design can be changed with the seasons or made permanent with a seal of protective film.

ABOVE: The rich tones of a walnut box are reflected in a display of deep bronze coloured Norway maple leaves.

MANY HAPPY RETURNS

Daisies
Lobelia
Meadowsweet
Queen Anne's lace (or any other
umbrella-like flowerheads)
Verbena
Sheet of lightweight green cardboard
Smaller piece of smooth white cardboard
Protective film
Latex adhesive
Ruler and pencil
Coloured felt-tip pen

Any child would be delighted to receive this pretty flower garden birthday card.

From the green cardboard cut a rectangle 24cm by 17.5cm (9½in by 7in) and fold it widthways. Cut out the birthday number from an offcut of green cardboard. From the white cardboard, cut out a rectangle 6.5cm by 12cm (2½in by 4¾in).

Place the number centrally at the base of the white card, then take a large spray of

ABOVE: Send 'Many Happy Returns' to a birthday child with this specially designed flower garden.

meadowsweet to make the large 'tree' top. Position a suitable stem for the trunk. Similarly, make a smaller tree for the other side of the number. Build up the picture by adding the other flowers to make a colourful garden 'border'. Cover the picture with protective film and trim to size.

Draw a suitable border in pencil on the green card to frame the white design card (the border shown above is an Edwardian 'reversed corner'). When you are satisfied with the design, go over it with a dark green felt-tip pen. Finally, fix the design card within the border.

LEFT: This selection of gift tags shows how versatile pressed flower designs can be. Use leftover pressings and cardboard scraps.

GIFT TAG SELECTION

Selection of pressed flowers and leaves
Offcuts of lightweight cardboard
Craft knife or scissors
Latex adhesive
Ribbon or cord
Hole punch
Marker pens and gold spray paint

Turn cardboard offcuts and leftover pressings into a selection of pretty gift tags. To make a basic card tag, cut a rectangle of cardboard to measure 3in by 4in (7.5cm by 10cm). Fold it in half widthways and punch holes at the top for the ribbon.

Thread the tags with different coloured ribbon or metallic cord and decorate them with leftover leaves and flowers. For added effect, draw on borders with marker pens or spray the leaves with gold paint.

BELOW: Gold spray paint shows off the delicacy of the cow parsley on these attractive little gift boxes.

BUTTERCUP CARD

Salad burnet (garden burnet)
Melilot
Buttercups
Sheet of firm green paper
Lightweight cream cardboard
Green marker pen
Ruler
Self-adhesive protective film
Craft knife
Latex adhesive

This buttercup card brings a ray of sunshine with its greeting and will give lasting pleasure if kept and framed.

Cut the green paper into a rectangle 2½in by 6½in (6.5cm by 16.5cm). Begin the arrangement with salad burnet and melilot, placing them in the top left corner and bringing them down to form a lazy V shape. Secure with tiny dabs of adhesive.

Add the buttercups towards the centre, saving the largest flowers for the focal point. For the best effect, tuck the leaves under the focal buttercup; also ensure that the V shape is not symmetrical.

Cover the design carefully with protective film and trim.

To make the rest of the card, cut a rectangle from the cream cardboard to measure 8in by 8½in (20cm by 21.5cm). Crease the cardboard and fold it in half lengthways.

ABOVE: Golden buttercups provide a treasured greeting card and one that can be kept long after the event.

Draw two rectangles to form a border for the design, making the outer rule twice as thick as the inner one. Finally, glue the design inside the border.

LITTLE BOXES

Cow parsley (alternatively, meadow parsley or wild carrot)
Two gift boxes
Latex adhesive
Gold spray paint

This is an extremely simple way to decorate little gift boxes and the results are stunning!

Remove the lid from one of the boxes and lightly secure three whole flowerheads of cow parsley diagonally across it. Using gold spray paint, give the top of the box two light coats of paint.

When the paint is dry, gently remove the cow parsley to reveal the unsprayed part of the box. This shows up as a pretty pattern through the paint.

Use the gold sprayed cow parsley to decorate the other box lid. Simply secure it to the lid with dabs of latex adhesive.

POT-POURRI

*Sweet-smelling rose petals form the basis of
many pot-pourri recipes.*

In days gone by, fresh herbs and flowers were
used to mask unpleasant odours and even keep
away disease. Gradually the first pot-pourris
were created and many fascinating and varied
recipes have been handed down over the years. So
instead of reaching for a synthetic room freshener,
try making your own pot-pourri to keep your
home fresh and fragrant.

There are two basic ways to make pot-pourri — the moist method and the dry method. It is possible to make both kinds yourself at home using either flowers from the garden or those you have bought.

Apart from the flowers, you will need a fixative to retain the plant's natural scent, which would otherwise quickly disappear. Powdered orris root, coarse, non-iodized salt, gum benzoin and spices such as cloves, cinnamon and nutmeg all act as fixatives. The final ingredient is essential oil, which is pure essence prepared from tons of scented flowers. This oil must be added very carefully, one drop at a time. Too much can ruin the delicate balance of your pot-pourri mixture, and you want to aim for a fragrance that is discernible but not overpowering.

All the additional ingredients needed to make your pot-pourri are readily available from natural health or beauty stores.

MOIST POT-POURRI

The original pot-pourris were made using the moist method. Although beautifully scented, this version does not have a naturally good colour and needs to be decorated with dried flowers or whole spices to make it look attractive when displayed in an open bowl.

The basic moist pot-pourri recipe uses partially dried scented rose petals. The petals are layered with coarse salt and, when ready, are mixed with herbs, spices, other scented petals and a fixative. A few drops of essential oil can be added to reinforce the scent.

Although this type of pot-pourri can take up to 12 weeks to prepare, the result will be more long-lasting and authentic than using the dry method.

Dried rose petals and lavender flowerheads are gathered to make dry pot-pourri. Whole spices, such as cinnamon bark, are used to fix the mixture and add a decorative touch.

DRY POT-POURRI

Nowadays, we mostly make a dry type of pot-pourri which involves drying flower petals fully and mixing them with dried leaves, spices and a fixative. A dry pot-pourri needs the addition of essential oils to boost the scent, which would not otherwise be as strong as that of the moist version. Always add the oil carefully, drop by drop, using a metal spoon rather than a wooden one which will absorb the oil itself.

The advantage of a dry pot-pourri is that it holds its colour and looks very pretty displayed in an open container. It also takes only four to six weeks to prepare.

DRYING FLOWERS

Drying your chosen flowers is easy. Choose healthy blooms picked on a dry day. Spread the petals or flowerheads out on to sheets of newspaper or wire cake-cooling racks and leave them in a warm and airy place to dry. If you leave the flowers on newspaper, you may need to turn them once or twice to ensure that all parts of the flower dry out. (Take care when drying individual petals as they can easily be blown away in a strong draught.)

It is best to dry herbs by hanging them in small bunches upside down — above a kitchen range (make sure they are out of the way of steam), in an airing cupboard or in a spare room, for example.

Orange and lemon peel (zest) should be dried naturally. You can do this by laying it out on absorbent kitchen paper and leaving it in a warm, dry place, such as an airing cupboard, for several days.

It will take from a few days to several weeks to dry the flowers or herbs, depending on the variety and where they have been left to dry. Individual petals will take less time than whole flowers or seedheads. (For more information see pages 35-39.)

MOIST POT-POURRI

10 cups of partially dried rose petals
3 cups of coarse salt
2 tbsp of ground cinnamon
2 tbsp of ground allspice
2 tbsp of ground nutmeg
1 tbsp of ground cloves
5 tbsp of orris root powder
3 or 4 drops of rose essential oil

This pot-pourri is made from roses only, but other scented flowers can be added with the spices. If you decide to do this, these additional flowers should always be fully dried.

The finished mixture is basically brown and not very attractive, but the scent is superb. Disguise the dull colour with a few whole roseheads.

The rose petals should be partially dried so that they feel leathery. Place some of the petals in a large bowl, cover them with a layer of coarse salt and continue to add layers of petals and salt until you have used up all the ingredients. Put a plate on top of the mixture in order to weigh it down. Stir the ingredients every day, to be sure that you are draining off any moisture.

After three to six weeks, crumble the mixture and add to it the spices, the rose essential oil and orris root powder. Seal the mix in paper bags and cure it for about six weeks before using.

Disguise the rather unappealing colours of Moist Pot-Pourri by piling it into a pretty basket, and adding whole, dried roseheads.

ABOVE: This attractive pink and red Rosebud pot-pourri is enhanced with cornflower petals and larkspur.

ROSEBUDS

4 cups of dried red or deep pink rose petals
1 cup of whole pink or red dried rosebuds
1 cup of dried lavender flowers
A few dried cornflower petals
Whole dried peonies (optional)
4 tbsp of orris root powder
1 tbsp of ground allspice
1 tbsp of ground cinnamon
1 tbsp of ground nutmeg
½ tbsp of ground cloves
4 or 5 drops of rose essential oil

Dried rosebuds are the perfect complement to a traditional rose petal pot-pourri mixture. For additional interest, add two or three larger blooms, such as open rose-heads or peonies.

Combine all the dry ingredients in a large bowl, sifting and mixing them well with your fingers. Stir in the orris root powder then, using a metal spoon, carefully add the rose essential oil.

Transfer the mixture to a sealed container and leave to cure in a cool, dark place for six weeks. Shake the mixture occasionally.

TRADITIONAL ROSE POT-POURRI

2 cups of dried strongly scented rose petals
1 cup of dried lavender
½ cup of dried marjoram
1 tbsp of cloves
½ cup of dried orange peel (zest)
6 nutmegs
3-4 broken cinnamon sticks
3 tbsp of orris root powder
4 or 5 drops of rose essential oil

This traditional English country recipe combines the wonderful fragrances of roses, orange and cinnamon.

Mix all the dried ingredients together in a large bowl. Add three tablespoons of orris root powder and stir thoroughly. Now carefully stir in the rose essential oil using a metal spoon. When the pot-pourri is well mixed put it into an airtight container and leave for four to six weeks, shaking the mixture occasionally.

RIGHT: Musky spices and deep-scented rose petals combine in this Traditional Rose Pot-Pourri.

ABOVE: Make little sachets from lacy handkerchiefs and fill them with this well-loved Original Lavender pot-pourri.

BELOW: Herbs and geranium are combined to form a subtle and aromatic pot-pourri.

ORIGINAL LAVENDER

4 cups of dried lavender flowers
2 cups of dried thyme
2 cups of dried lemon mint (Mentha x piperita citrata) leaves
A few dried blue borage (Borago) flowers
½ cup of coarse salt
1 tbsp of powdered cloves
1 tbsp of caraway seeds
1 tbsp of dried lemon peel (zest)
3 or 4 drops of lavender essential oil

Lavender must be one of the best known and best loved of all scents. This simple pot-pourri mixture is absolutely ideal for filling sachets to keep clothes and linen fresh and sweet.

Gather your ingredients together and tear some of the larger leaves into smaller pieces. Place the dry ingredients in a large bowl and mix them thoroughly, making sure the salt is combined. Carefully add a few drops of lavender essential oil. Stir again, then pour into airtight containers and store the mix for about six weeks, giving the container an occasional shake.

HERB AND GERANIUM

1 cup of dried scented geranium leaves
1 cup of dried marjoram and oregano flowers
1 cup of dried mint leaves and flowers
1 cup of dried blue cornflowers
2 tbsp of orris root powder
3 drops of rose geranium essential oil

This purple-blue mixture looks so pretty in a piece of blue and white china.

Remove any remaining stalks from the flowers and leaves, then gently mix the ingredients together in a large bowl. Add the orris root powder and mix thoroughly. Now drop in the essential oil very carefully. Stir the mixture well and put into an airtight container for four to six weeks, shaking it occasionally.

MEADOWSWEET

2 cups of dried pink and cream helichrysum (strawflowers)
2 cups of dried pink rose petals
2 cups of dried mint leaves
1 cup of dried thyme and sage leaves, mixed
1 cup of dried marjoram and meadowsweet, mixed
1 cup of dried deep pink statice flowers
1 cup of dried rose geranium leaves and flowers
1 cup of dried elderflowers
½ cup of dried buchu leaves
1 tbsp of dried lemon peel (zest)
5 tbsp of powdered orris root
5 or 6 drops of patchouli essential oil

Meadowsweet is a pretty recipe, and looks charming in low baskets with handfuls of helichrysum (strawflowers) and statice strewn on top. Blend the dried flowers and herbs in a mixing bowl. Add lemon peel, orris root and patchouli essential oil. Stir thoroughly and keep in an airtight container for six weeks, shaking occasionally.

RIGHT: Meadowsweet is a wonderful country mixture with a sweet, earthy scent.

BURNING BUNDLES

Stalks from dried lavender, rosemary,
thyme and lemon verbena
Twigs
Pine or larch cones, preferably still
on their twigs
String

Although not strictly pot-pourri, these bundles of aromatic twigs, stalks and cones scent the room beautifully when burned on an open fire. They make good use of the stripped stalks you might have left over from making more traditional pot-pourri. Scattered across the fireplace or stored in open baskets, they look most attractive.

Gather the aromatic stalks, twigs and cones into small bundles and tie them with pieces of string. Hang them up or place them in shallow baskets close to the fire.

FOREST WALK

3 cups of well-dried pinewood shavings
3 cups of small pine cones
2 cups of mixed nuts
1 cup of acorns, well dried
1 cup of cinnamon bark
1 cup of dried golden rod or yellow statice
2 tsp of dried orange peel (zest)
½ cup of bay leaves
1 tsp of mixed spice
5 tbsp of orris root powder
6 or 8 drops of pine essential oil

This mixture will fill your room with an invigorating pine fragrance. Bowls of this pot-pourri can look very effective when displayed with a handful of acorns and yellow flowerheads scattered on top.

Before you begin, check that all your ingredients are completely dried out. This applies especially to the wood shavings and the acorns which could attract mildew

LEFT: Fragrant twigs and sticks are gathered into Burning Bundles ready to be placed on an open fire.

ABOVE: The chunky textures and woodland tones of Forest Walk create a more masculine pot-pourri – perfect for a study or bedroom.

mould if they are not thoroughly dry. Discard anything if it shows any trace of damp before you prepare the pot-pourri.

Mix all the dried items together in a large bowl. Next, add two or three drops of pine essential oil. Mix well, then transfer to dry airtight containers for six weeks, shaking occasionally while the mixture is curing.

NATURE'S FRUITS

1 cup of peach stones
1 cup of rose hips
1 cup of beech masts (nuts)
1 cup of larch cones
1 cup of star anise
3 or 4 whole or cracked nutmegs
6 broken cinnamon sticks
1 cup of dried apple slices
4 tbsp of orris root powder
3 drops of allspice essential oil
3 drops of sweet orange essential oil

This wintery mixture of spices, cones and fruit makes an unusual pot-pourri. You can dry the apple slices by placing them on a baking sheet and leaving them for several hours at the bottom of an oven set at a very low temperature.

With the exception of the apples, orris root and oil, mix all the ingredients together in a large bowl. Add the orris root powder to the mixture and stir in the essential oil, drop by drop. When the ingredients are thoroughly mixed, stir in the apple. Place the pot-pourri in an airtight container for about a month, shaking it regularly.

BELOW: The fruit and spice mix of Nature's Fruits looks best displayed in a shallow bowl.

ABOVE: The shells used in Ocean Fragrance can be collected from the beach or bought from a shell or craft shop.

BELOW: Spring Selection has plenty of whole flowerheads for texture, including roses, marigolds, mimosa and helichrysum (strawflowers). For interest, add a bunch of cinnamon sticks.

OCEAN FRAGRANCE

1 cup of assorted shells
½ cup of dried oak moss
6 cinnamon sticks
1 cup of dried blue larkspur flowers
A few love-in-the-mist seedheads
and beech masts (nuts)
2 tbsp of orris root powder
4 drops of essential oil of your choice

Perfect for any bathroom, this seashell pot-pourri can be scented just as you wish, although a spicy or woody fragrance is probably more suitable than a floral one.

Place all the dried ingredients and the shells into a large bowl and mix them together well. Add the orris root powder and mix in. Finally, add the essential oil and stir in until all the oil is absorbed.

Put the mixture into an airtight container and leave for four to six weeks, giving it an occasional shake.

SPRING SELECTION

1 cup of dried chamomile flowers
½ cup of dried marigold petals
½ cup of dried lemon verbena leaves
1 cup of dried mixed yellow flowers,
eg mimosa, tulip, daffodil
A few whole dried yellow chilli peppers,
marigold heads or cinnamon
sticks for decoration
2 tsp of ground coriander
2 tsp of ground cinnamon
2 tbsp of orris root powder
4 drops of vetivert essential oil

This light, lemony, pot-pourri will give you a delightful mixture for spring.

Mix the petals, flowers and leaves in a large bowl. Add the spices and orris root, stirring well. Drip the essential oil into the mixture, and stir well with a metal spoon. Put into a sealed container, and leave for four to six weeks, shaking occasionally.

ABOVE: A traditional rose petal pot-pourri, Sweet Rose is made in a slightly unusual way using aromatic vanilla pods.

SWEET ROSE

6 cups of strong scented dried rose petals
6 dried bay leaves – finely chopped
4 dried vanilla pods
2 tbsp of coarse salt
1 tbsp of ground nutmeg
1 tbsp of orris root powder
1 tbsp of powdered cinnamon
A large screw-top jar

This pot-pourri is made by a slightly different method, even though it uses all dried ingredients. The addition of the vanilla pods gives the pot-pourri an exotic and unusual aroma.

Set aside the vanilla pods and 1 tablespoon of the coarse salt, and mix all the other ingredients together well. Place the vanilla pods round the inside edge of the jar in an upright position. Now fill the jar with layers of your mixture, sprinkling the remaining salt between each layer. Finish with a final layer of salt on top. Secure the jar tightly and leave it undisturbed for at least a month.

HERBAL DELIGHT

1 cup of dried lavender flowers
½ cup of dried mint
½ cup of dried marjoram
½ cup of dried oregano flowers
1 cup of dried lemon verbena
2 tbsp of orris root powder
3 or 4 drops of lavender essential oil

Herbs have always been renowned for their restorative and relaxing properties. The combined scents of dried herbs and lavender create a soothing mixture, ideal for a bedroom or bathroom.

Mix all the dried ingredients together in a large bowl, then add two tablespoons of orris root powder. Carefully add the lavender essential oil, one drop at a time, and mix it in thoroughly using a metal spoon.

Finally, place the mixture in an airtight container and leave it to mature for four to six weeks in a cool, dark place. Shake the mixture occasionally.

ABOVE: An aromatic and soothing pot-pourri, Herbal Delight emits a wonderfully subtle fragrance.

 95

SANDALWOOD BOX

1 cup of whole dried yellow rose heads
1 cup of whole dried marigold heads
½ cup of mixed dried bay and
lemon verbena leaves
½ cup of mixed dried yellow petals and
flowers, such as helichrysum (strawflowers),
dahlia, or achillea
Larch cones and beech masts (nuts)
3 tbsp of orris root powder
1 tbsp of dried lemon peel (zest)

1 tbsp each of cinnamon, cloves and nutmeg
3 drops of sandalwood essential oil

An antique box or old-fashioned tea caddy makes a perfect container in which to keep and display this golden, wood-fragrant pot-pourri. Add just a few larch cones and beech masts (nuts) or whole flowerheads for a finishing touch.

Mix the petals, flowers and leaves together in a large bowl. Stir in the spices, lemon peel (zest) and orris root powder and mix well. Now add the essential oil, drop by drop, stirring it well with a metal spoon.

Put the mixture into a sealed container, and place somewhere cool and dry. Leave to mature for four to six weeks, shaking the container occasionally.

A tiny tea chest makes an ideal container for a desktop pot-pourri such as Sandalwood Box. It can be kept closed mostly, keeping the scent in, and opened when the desk is in use.

SPICE BOWL

1 cup of dried lemon verbena leaves
½ cup of dried rose petals
1 cup of whole coriander seeds
1 tbsp of allspice berries
6 whole nutmegs
1 tbsp of whole star anise
1 tbsp of crushed cinnamon bark
1 tsp each of ground nutmeg and coriander
2 tbsp of orris root powder
4 drops of cedarwood essential oil

Old storage tins designed for spices and other kitchen ingredients look good filled with a suitably spicy pot-pourri such as this one. This recipe produces a rather masculine fragrance — clean and slightly exotic.

Place the dried leaves and petals into a large bowl and stir together. Add the orris

BELOW: This Spice Bowl pot-pourri mixture is displayed in an old canister, possibly once used for storing spices.

ABOVE: This golden, spicy Marigold Mix is decorated with preserved yellow roses and cinnamon sticks.

root powder and spices and mix again. Now add the drops of essential oil very carefully, mixing everything together with a metal spoon.

Put the mixture into a sealed container and leave to mature for four to six weeks, shaking the contents occasionally.

MARIGOLD MIX

1 cup of dried marigold flowers
4 or 5 yellow roseheads
4 or 5 broken cinnamon sticks
1 tbsp of cloves
1 tbsp of star anise
1 tbsp of allspice berries
2 tbsp of small eucalyptus leaves
1 tbsp of orris root powder
3 or 4 drops of cinnamon or allspice
essential oil

This golden pot-pourri smells as good as it looks! You can either add a few dried yellow roseheads for the finishing touch, or use several whole marigold heads.

Place the marigolds, spices and leaves in a large bowl and mix them well with a large metal spoon. Add the orris root powder and stir the mixture thoroughly.

Carefully add the essential oil, drop by drop, stir the mixture, then place it in an airtight container for four to six weeks, shaking it occasionally.

Presenting Pot-Pourri

The different ways of displaying and using pot-pourris are endless. At first you may simply want to display your newly made pot-pourri in a large bowl, but it is worth considering other ways of presenting it.

Large containers made from wood, metal or ceramic are all suitable, enabling you to spread out the ingredients and appreciate fully the beauty of the different flowers and leaves as well as the delicious scents.

There are also many other ways of presenting your pot-pourri. Baskets lined with pretty fabric make attractive containers, especially if you tuck dried flowerheads into the rim, for example.

Boxes are another good idea. A polished wood box or a prettily papered cardboard box creates the perfect foil for a mixture of colourful petals (see page 146).

Or use an illustrated biscuit or kitchen tin. The lid can be replaced occasionally to preserve the scent of the pot-pourri.

ABOVE: An antique tea cup and saucer play the perfect host to a colourful pot-pourri.

RIGHT: Pot-pourri can be layered in glass, colour by colour, for an effective result.

ABOVE: This simple wooden box, filled with pot-pourri, has a handful of dried poppy seedheads glued firmly to the lid for a handle and decoration all in one.

TEA PARTY

Antique china provides the perfect setting for many pot-pourris. Sugar bowls and large cups that no longer belong to a service are ideal, and they can be found quite cheaply in antique markets and junk shops.

BOXING CLEVER

Plain, undecorated wooden boxes make ideal containers for pot-pourri. They can be painted, stencilled, varnished or sprayed. A clever idea is to gather small clusters of dried flowers or seedheads and glue them on to the lid. Poppy seedheads look lovely left their natural, sculptured greyish green. Alternatively, spray them gold or silver.

GOOD IN GLASS

Clear glass is not usually very sympathetic with the texture of dried petals and leaves, but layering different coloured flowers in simple modern glass containers such as tanks and cylinders can look wonderful, particularly in a modern setting.

ABOVE: Transform an ordinary cardboard box with colourful, stripy wallpaper which echoes the petals of the pot-pourri. Alternatively, use an attractive floral wallpaper.

 98

FLOWERS AS FOOD

*Edible flowers make wonderful decorative
features on spring and summertime
puddings, cakes or sweets.*

Garnishing food with flowers and herbs has long
been popular, but many recipes in this chapter
use flowers as a major ingredient as well. The
final results are extremely good and the subtle
flavours and textures that flowers can introduce
to a dish suit the modern move towards light,
simple tastes and fresh, natural food.

*M*ost gardens, whatever their size, will provide enough space to grow a selection of flowers for the kitchen. Thyme, hyssop and mint can all be used for their leaves as well as their flowers. Nasturtiums and marigolds are superb in salads and they add a splash of brilliant colour and a delicious spicy flavour. (The marigolds used in the recipes in this chapter are *Calendula officinalis* and not the African marigold, *Tagetes*.) Roses can be used in summer puddings to add a subtle aroma as well as a pretty garnish.

Make sure that the flowers you use for your recipes are fresh, unblemished and unsprayed. Check for insects and, if you wash the flowerheads, do so carefully as the delicate petals can bruise easily.

If you decide to experiment with different types of flowers, do check first that they are edible, as some flowers are poisonous. It is important to follow the instructions closely in this chapter, and not to eat more than the amount specified in the recipes.

Remember, too, that some wild flowers are scarce, so only pick common species, growing in abundance.

CRYSTALLIZING FLOWERS

There are various methods of making crystallized flowers, but only two of these are useful to the home cook. One method is for a quick effect only, while the other makes flowers that will last for several months. Both methods produce very pretty and delicious results.

Primroses, violets, rose petals, lavender and honeysuckle are all suitable.

Quick method
1 egg white
Caster (superfine) sugar

Lightly beat the egg white until it is bubbly but not frothy. Paint this on to the petals with an artist's soft brush, making sure to coat every part of the flower.

Dip the flowers into the caster sugar and gently shake off any surplus sugar. Leave the flowers to dry in a warm place. When they have hardened they are ready for use.

Longer lasting method
1 tbsp of gum arabic
1 tbsp of rosewater
Caster (superfine) sugar

Gum arabic is available from chemists. It is quite expensive, but only a little is needed to preserve a batch of flowers. Dissolve the gum arabic in the rosewater and leave it until it has become a thick paste. Paint this on to the petals, leaving no gaps. Dip the flowers into the caster sugar and leave them in a warm place until crisp and dry. The crystallized flowers can be stored in an airtight container until ready for use.

Primroses are among the best flowers for crystallizing. Here they have been used with violets to decorate a cake and some fondants.

ABOVE: Water melon is infused with borage and decorated with scented geranium.

GERANIUM MELON

Small water melon
½ pt (300ml / 1¼ cups) of water
2½ oz (75g / ⅓ cup) of caster (superfine) sugar
Juice of 1 lemon and 1 lime
Strips of lemon peel (zest)
Borage (Borago) leaves and flowers
Scented geranium flowers

This colourful combination makes a wonderfully refreshing starter or dessert.

Extract the fruit from the water melon and remove the pips. Then chop the melon into rough cubes.

Mix together the water, sugar, lemon peel and borage leaves and add the melon cubes. Simmer for a few minutes to combine the flavours, strain and allow to cool. Add the lemon and lime juice and put the mixture back into the scooped-out melon.

SUMMER SALAD

Mixed lettuce leaves
Nasturtium, cornflower and borage
(Borago) flowerheads
Dill
Dressing:
2 tbsp of olive oil
1 tbsp of walnut oil
1 tsp of made French mustard
1 tbsp of white wine vinegar
Salt and ground pepper

This attractive salad, rich in vitamin C, can be eaten as a first course or on its own.

The flowers should be fresh, unblemished and unsprayed. If possible, do not wash them, as the petals bruise easily. Check for insects and pick the flowerheads off the stems. Mix the nasturtiums and other flowers with the lettuce leaves.

To make the dressing, put all the ingredients together in a screw-top jar and shake vigorously. Carefully toss the dressing with the salad just before serving.

MIXED CHICORY SALAD

1 small oak leaf lettuce
1 small cos lettuce
A few leaves of frisée
1 head of Belgian chicory
1 small red radicchio
Vinaigrette
Chicory flowers

Wild chicory or succory (*Cichorium intybus*) and its commercially grown varieties — such as Belgian chicory — bears beautiful sky blue, and sometimes pink, flowers. It has a delicious bitter taste which transforms ordinary leafy salads. Another type of chicory, *Cichorium endivia,* is more commonly known as endive or frisée; it has a red cultivar called radiccio. This salad combines several chicory types.

Wash and dry the leaves of the lettuce and the various chicories. Arrange them in a salad bowl and toss with a sweetish vinaigrette. Decorate with blue chicory flowers. **Serves 6-8.**

ABOVE: Nasturtiums are among the easiest perennials to grow. Eaten when freshly picked, they make a dazzling Summer Salad.

RIGHT: Chicory adds a bitterness to salads which enlivens the taste dramatically. The blue flowers provide an attractive contrast.

BORAGE SOUP

*½ lb (250g) of young borage (Borago) leaves
and flowers
2oz (60g / ⅓ cup) of short grain rice
2oz (60g / ¼ cup) of butter
1½ pt (900ml / 3¾ cups) of chicken or
vegetable stock
6oz (175g / ¾ cup) of thick cream
Seasoning to taste*

This dark green soup is served cold and makes an ideal starter to a summer dinner party or extra special picnic.

Melt the butter in a saucepan and add the rice. Cook over a low heat for two minutes, stirring all the time. Add the stock and simmer for 15 minutes.

Strip the borage leaves and flowers from the stalks and wash well. Leave aside some flowers for decoration and add the remainder to the saucepan. Simmer for a further 10 minutes. Season to taste.

Allow the soup to cool for a while, then liquidize it in a blender. Pour the soup through a sieve or strainer into a serving dish and allow to cool.

Before serving, stir in the cream or, if preferred, you could try some thinned fromage frais. Decorate with borage flowers. **Serves 4.**

MARIGOLD CAULIFLOWER

*1 medium sized cauliflower
2oz (60g / ¼ cup) of butter
2oz (60g / ½ cup) of plain white flour
3oz (90g / ⅓ cup) of grated cheese
½ pt (300ml / 1¼ cups) of milk
6 marigold (Calendula officinalis)
flowerheads
Salt and pepper*

Marigolds are extremely bright and cheerful flowers, and they can be very good to

LEFT: *A delicious chilled green soup made from borage and decorated with the plant's pretty flowers makes an ideal summer starter.*

ABOVE: *Transform cauliflower cheese with deliciously fragrant marigold petals.*

eat. They have a subtle, spicy flavour which transforms this classic cauliflower dish into something special.

Make the white sauce in the usual way. Carefully wash the marigold flowers in cold running water and shake dry. Reheat the sauce and stir in the grated cheese, but do not allow to boil. Remove the pan from the heat and stir in the marigold petals. Place the cooked cauliflower into a serving dish and pour the sauce over the top. **Serves 4.**

PRIMROSE AND POTATO SALAD

*1½ lb (750g) of new potatoes, cooked
and cooled
½ lb (250g) of french beans, cooked and cooled
1 yellow sweet pepper (capsicum or
bell pepper)
Lettuce leaves
Primrose flowers and foliage
Dressing:
4 tbsp of salad oil
1 tbsp of lemon juice
1 clove of garlic
1 tsp of honey
Seasoning to taste*

In springtime, primroses can make a pretty and colourful addition to a potato salad.

To make the dressing, simply shake all the ingredients together in a screw-top jar.

For the salad, wash and de-seed the sweet pepper and cut into fine strips. Chop three french beans into small pieces for the top of the salad. Then mix the potatoes, remaining beans and peppers together with the dressing.

Line a bowl with lettuce and primrose leaves and fill it with the potato salad. Decorate the top of the salad with primrose flowers and french beans.

A beautiful medley of springtime colours uses primrose flowers and leaves.

RIGHT: Aromatic thyme lends a wonderful flavour to grilled chicken. The flowering sprigs create the perfect decoration.

CHICKEN AND THYME

4 skinned chicken breasts
Long stems of thyme in bloom
Bunch of fresh thyme leaves
3 tbsp of corn oil
Juice of 2 lemons
Salt and pepper

Chicken cooked with thyme tastes absolutely delicious and this appetizing dish is the perfect choice for an informal summer lunch or barbecue party.

Chop or grind the bunch of thyme and mix in a large bowl with the oil, lemon juice and seasoning. Add the chicken pieces to the mixture and leave to marinate for two hours, turning the chicken occasionally.

Remove the chicken just before cooking and allow it to drain, but make sure that you leave plenty of the chopped thyme on the chicken pieces.

Cook the chicken over a medium hot barbecue for approximately 20 minutes. For extra flavour, dip the flowering thyme into the marinade and lay it over the chicken while the underside is cooking. Reserve some for decoration.
Serves 4.

MARIGOLD FILLETS

4 fillets of smoked mackerel or herring
Small green lettuce
Sauce:
2 tbsp of sunflower oil
4 tbsp of cider vinegar
2 heaped tsp of grated horseradish
8 marigold (Calendula officinalis)
flowerheads

Serve succulent smoked mackerel or herring fillets on a bed of orange marigold flowers and crisp green lettuce for a winning summer party dish.

Pour the vinegar into a mixing bowl, add the horseradish and crush well with a wooden spoon. Blend in the sunflower oil and leave to infuse for 30 minutes.

Wash the flowers and drain well. Cut the fish fillets in half lengthways and arrange in a star shape on a bed of lettuce.

Finally, stir the marigold petals into the sauce and spoon some of it over the dish. Reserve the remainder to serve separately.
Serves 4.

ABOVE: Bright green lettuce and orange marigolds frame a star of smoked fish fillets.

MARIGOLD MUSTARD

2 tbsp of dried marigold (Calendula officinalis) flowers
8oz (225g) pot of strong, grainy mustard

This unusual mustard is excellent served with cold pork or ham.

Finely chop the marigolds and put them into a mixing bowl. Add the whole jar of mustard and mix thoroughly, making sure that the flowers are well distributed.

Spoon the mustard into a suitable container (you can wash the original mustard container and soak off the label if it's an attractive jar). Seal the jar and add a label or little yellow ribbon if you wish.

RIGHT: This recipe uses spicy marigold petals to jazz up a plain, grainy mustard.

PINK PEARS

6 firm pears
½ bottle of red wine
2 tbsp of brown sugar
18 garden pinks (Dianthus x allwoodii)
½ pt (300ml / 1¼ cups) of thick cream
2 tbsp of milk
Sugar to taste

This elegant dish is perfect for a dinner party dessert.

Wash the pinks carefully and shake them to dry. Remove the petals from 12 of the flowers and place in a saucepan with the wine and sugar. Bring this to the boil.

Peel the pears but leave them on their stalks. Place in the saucepan with the wine and sugar solution and leave to simmer for 20 minutes, turning them so that all the sides colour evenly. Remove the pears and reduce the liquid by boiling rapidly to make a thick sauce. Allow to cool.

To make the cream accompaniment, heat the milk in a double saucepan and add the petals from the remaining flowers. Heat to just below boiling point for 5 minutes. Remove from the heat and allow this to stand for 15 minutes for the flavours to combine before straining the milk into a bowl. Add a teaspoon of sugar, allow to dissolve, then pour in the thick cream and beat to a stiff consistency.

Serve the pears standing upright in a puddle of wine sauce. The cream mixture can be served separately.
Serves 6

LEFT: *Fragrant garden pinks are added to a pear sauce and cream accompaniment to create a deliciously rich yet refreshing dessert.*

ROSE PETAL SORBET

1 large cup of rose petals
4oz (125g / ½ cup) of caster (superfine) sugar
15fl oz (450ml / scant 2 cups) of water
Pared rind (zest) and juice of 2 lemons
1 egg white

This deliciously refreshing sorbet can be made with a variety of flowers (see below).

Dissolve the sugar in the water and add the lemon rind. Bring to the boil, stirring continuously, then simmer for 6 minutes. Add the rose petals, remove from the heat and allow to cool.

Strain the mixture, then add the lemon juice, tasting as you go so as not to mask the flower flavour.

Freeze in a plastic container for 2 to 3 hours. When mushy and half frozen, add the stiffly beaten egg white and continue to beat. If you do this in a food processor, the result will be very fluffy and snowlike.

Freeze again until firm. Allow to soften slightly before serving.
Serves 6.

These truffles are flavoured with roses or violets and decorated with crystallized petals.

SORBET VARIATIONS

Instead of rose-flavoured sorbet you can make other varieties. Simply replace the rose petals in the recipe above with any one of the following: 6 flowering sprigs of lavender; 2 large heads of elderflower; 4 leaves of scented geranium; 12 sprigs of herbs. You can also replace the sugar with 2½ oz (75g/⅓ cup) of honey.

TRUFFLES

6oz (175g) of white or plain (bittersweet)
chocolate (for centres)
2 tbsp of single (light) cream
1 egg yolk
1 tbsp of brandy and 1 tbsp of rosewater
or 2 tbsp of violet liqueur
6oz (175g) of white or plain (bittersweet)
chocolate (for coating)
Crystallized petals

Scented rose petal or lavender sorbets make fragrant, delicious desserts for those long, hot summer days.

These delicious truffles are made from the same basic mixture, but the rose version has a dark rose-scented, brandy truffle centre covered with white chocolate, and the violet version has a white, violet-scented centre encased in plain chocolate.

Begin by gently melting the chocolate for the centres into the cream. Add the egg yolk, flavouring and liqueur. Remove from the heat and allow to cool.

Next, roll the mixture into little balls and leave them to harden. Melt the coating chocolate gently over hot water and dip each truffle in until well coated. Leave the truffles on an oiled surface and, to finish, decorate them with crystallized petals before they have set.
Makes about 15

 109

NECTARINE AND BORAGE SALAD

4 nectarines
Juice of half a lemon or lime
Fresh borage (Borago) flowers

At the height of summer, when fruit is at its best and most plentiful, make a simple fruit salad with borage.

Wash the nectarines and slice them into thin segments. They look best with the deep red skin left on the orange flesh.

Layer the nectarine slices in a deep bowl, adding a sprinkling of lime or lemon juice. Scatter the borage flowers over the fruit and serve immediately. Peaches can be substituted for nectarines.
Serves 4.

ELDERFLOWER CHEESECAKE

8oz (250g / 2 cups) of crushed digestive
biscuits (Graham crackers)
2oz (50g / ¼ cup) of melted butter
8oz (250g / 1 cup) of cream cheese
2 eggs, separated
4 tbsp of Greek set yoghurt
2 tbsp of honey
Handful of chopped elderflowers
2oz (50g / ½ cup) of sultanas (golden
raisins) soaked overnight in
3 tbsp of elderflower wine
4fl oz (100ml / scant ½ cup) of thick cream

Elderflowers add a tasty tang to this delicious cheesecake. First, mix the crushed biscuits with the melted butter, and press the mixture into the base of an 8in (20cm) loose-bottomed baking tin.

Beat the butter and honey together, then beat in the egg yolks. Next mix in the cream cheese, the wine and sultanas. Beat the egg whites until stiff and fold into the mixture. Pour into the biscuit-lined baking tin and cook in a moderate oven for 40 minutes. Set aside to cool.

To decorate, whip the thick cream until it is stiff, adding a little sugar to taste if you like. Put the cream into a piping bag (pastry bag) and, using a fluted nozzle, pipe cream around the edge of the cheesecake.

This simple dish of sliced nectarines is liberally sprinkled with edible, star-shaped borage flowers.

STUFFED NASTURTIUMS

2oz (50g / ¼ cup) of granulated sugar
6oz (175g / ¾ cup) of ricotta cheese
1 drop of pure almond essence
4oz (100g / ⅔ cup) of blanched almonds,
finely chopped
4fl oz (100ml / scant ½ cup) of thick cream,
stiffly whipped
16 nasturtium flowers

This recipe makes a pretty and delicious summer pudding.

Gather the flowers when they are fresh and have just fully opened. Avoid washing them if possible, but do ensure that they are unblemished and are free from pesticides and insects.

Lightly beat the sugar into the cheese and when the sugar has dissolved add the almond essence to the mixture. Toast the chopped almonds in a hot oven, watching carefully so they do not burn. Remove, and leave them to cool.

Fold the whipped cream into the cheese mixture and add the toasted almonds to it. Then taste and adjust the sweetening and the flavouring. Take small spoonfuls of the mixture and stuff each flower. Serve with a colourful fresh fruit salad or a fruit sauce. *Serves 4.*

ABOVE: A traditional baked cheesecake is enlivened with tangy elderflower.

BELOW: Offer guests this tasty pudding made from nasturtium flowers filled with cream cheese and crunchy toasted almonds.

VIOLET SPONGE

4 eggs
4oz (125g / 1 cup) of self-raising
(all-purpose) flour
4oz (125g / ½ cup) of sugar
1oz (25g / 1 tbsp) of melted butter
8fl oz (25ml / 1 cup) of thick cream
2 tbsp of violet liqueur (see page 117)
Bunch of violets

Violets add a subtle fragrance and a delicate taste to this traditional sponge cake. First, brush two 7in (18cm) baking tins with oil and line the base of the tins with oiled greaseproof paper.

Place a bowl containing the eggs and sugar over a pan of hot water and, using an electric whisk, beat fast until the mixture becomes thick and fluffy, and will hold the impression of the whisk. Sift in a quarter of the flour and fold in with a metal spoon. Gradually fold in the remainder of the flour, and lastly the cooled melted butter.

Immediately turn the mixture out into the baking tins and bake in a fairly hot oven (190°C/375°F/gas mark 5) for about 30 minutes. Turn out on to a wire rack to cool. When cold drizzle violet liqueur over each sponge base.

BELOW: This fabulous sponge cake is made in the traditional way and drizzled with a little delicious violet liqueur. The rich, deep purple of the fresh violets are the perfect decoration.

For the filling, beat the cream and reserve two tablespoons for piping. Spread the remaining cream over one of the sponges and place the other sponge on top.

Pipe rosettes of cream around the edge of the filling and make a garland of rosettes on the top of the cake.

Finally, carefully wash and dry the violets, and cut away the bracts. Push the flowers into the cream around the filling and pile the remaining violets in the centre of the cream garland.

MARIGOLD CAKE

8oz (250g / 1 cup) of softened butter
8oz (250g / 1 cup) of caster (superfine) sugar
4 eggs, beaten
8oz (250g / 2 cups) of self-raising
(all-purpose) flour
Grated rind (zest) of 1 orange and 1 lemon
3 tbsp of fresh marigold (Calendula officinalis) petals or 2 tbsp of dried
Granulated sugar (optional)

Marigold petals give a delicate flavour and a slight orange hue to this deliciously light tea-time cake.

First, grease and line a 2lb (1kg) loaf tin. Cream the butter together with the sugar and add the beaten egg a little at a time. Sieve the flour with the baking powder and fold into the creamed mixture. Stir in the orange and lemon rinds and the petals.

Spoon the mixture into the tin and bake in a preheated oven 350°F (180°C or gas mark 4) for about 1 hour. Sprinkle with granulated sugar about halfway through the cooking time if desired. Cool for 5 minutes, then remove from the tin. Serve when just cool.
Serves 8/10

RIGHT: This delicious cake is made from a traditional sponge recipe with fresh marigold petals added to give a subtle flavour.

ABOVE: Capture summer scents and flavours with this delicious lemon-geranium and apple preserve.

GERANIUM PRESERVE

*4lb (2kg) of cooking apples
1¾ pt (1 litre) of water
Granulated or preserving sugar
Juice of 2 lemons
15 scented geranium leaves*

Scented geraniums are wonderfully old-fashioned plants. Their leaves smell of rose, lemon, eucalyptus, ginger, lime, balsam and orange. The lemon- or rose-scented leaves make the most delicious preserves.

Chop the apples roughly, leaving the skin, stalks and pips. Put in a large pan with the water and simmer until soft. Strain for several hours through a jelly bag or muslin; do not squeeze the fruit pulp through or the preserve will be cloudy.

Measure the juice into a preserving pan and for every pint (600ml) of juice add 1lb (450g) of sugar. Add the lemon juice and the geranium leaves. Stir over a low heat, then boil rapidly until set, for about 10 minutes. Quickly remove the leaves and pour into clean, warm jars. Cover while still hot.

Serve with home-made bread or plain scones. Alternatively, use as a filling for a sponge cake, reserving some leaves and petals for decoration.

ROSE HIP JELLY

*1lb (450g) of cooking apples, unpeeled and quartered
2lb (900g) of rose hips, roughly chopped
2pt (1 litre) of water
Juice of 1 lemon
Granulated sugar*

Rose hips are ripe from late summer to autumn and can be preserved in this lovely jelly. The result is sharp and fruity with a beautiful garnet colour.

Put the apples and rose hips into a large saucepan and pour over the water to just cover. Boil gently for about 1 hour, until the fruit is very soft.

Pour into a jelly bag or a square of muslin and hang up to drip over a large bowl. Do not press the fruit pulp or the jelly will be cloudy. Leave overnight.

The next day, measure out the drained juice and, for every pint (600ml) of juice, measure 1lb (450g) of sugar. Put the juice and sugar into a saucepan and heat slowly

BELOW: This golden honey is delicately flavoured with lavender.

ABOVE: Rose hip jelly has a wonderful garnet glow. It tastes fruity and sharp.

until the sugar has dissolved. Now, boil rapidly for about 10 minutes until a setting point is reached.

Skim any foam from the surface and pour into hot, sterilized jars. When cool, seal the jars in the usual way. This jelly is delicious served with roast lamb or game.
Makes about 1½-2lb (700-900g)

LAVENDER HONEY

Small jar of runny honey
Handful of fresh lavender flowers
Small bunch of lavender to decorate

This delicately flavoured honey is so easy to prepare and makes an attractive gift.

Warm the honey and lavender flowers in a heatproof bowl over a saucepan of simmering water for about 15 minutes. Do not allow the honey to boil.

Strain the honey through a fine sieve and discard the lavender flowers. Pour into a sterilized jar and, when cool, seal. Decorate the jar with a sprig of lavender flowers and a little pale mauve ribbon.

ROSE PETAL JELLY

4lb (2kg) of cooking apples
2pts (1 litre) of water
Juice of 2 lemons
Granulated or preserving sugar
1pt (600ml) scented rose petals

Rose petals make a delicious, sweet jelly. However, by themselves they can be rather cloying, so it is best to make a sharp-flavoured base from apples or redcurrants.

Chop the apples, leaving the skin stalks and pips. Put in a large pan with the water and simmer until soft. Put into a jelly bag and strain for several hours (don't squeeze the pulp as this will make the jelly cloudy).

Measure the juice into a preserving pan and for every pint (600ml) of juice add 1lb (450g) of sugar. Add the lemon juice and rose petals. Stir over a low heat to dissolve the sugar then boil rapidly for about 10 minutes until it sets. Remove the petals and pour the jelly into clean, warm jars. Cover while still hot and label.
Makes about 4lb/2kg

RIGHT: Rose petal jelly turns plain bread and scones into a special tea-time treat.

CLARET PUNCH

1 tbsp of caster (superfine) sugar
8oz (250g) of fresh strawberries
Small strips of cucumber peel
Juice of 3 lemons
3 tbsp of brandy
2 tbsp of Cointreau or orange liqueur
2 bottles of claret or similar red wine

1 bottle of sparkling mineral water,
soda or lemonade
Borage (Borago) flowers and mint

This delicious cherry-red wine cup is best served from a clear glass bowl to appreciate the sparkling colour and pretty decoration. Dissolve the sugar in a little hot water and pour into a large bowl. Slice the strawber-ries if they are large and add to the bowl together with the cucumber strips, lemon juice, brandy and Cointreau. Pour in the red wine and top up with the sparkling water, soda or lemonade. Chill well.

When the punch is ready to serve, add ice and decorate it with a liberal sprinkling of borage flowers and mint sprigs.
Serves 20.

VIOLET LIQUEUR

18fl oz (500ml / 2 cups) of vodka
50 heads of scented Parma violets
7oz (200g / ¾ cup) white sugar
¼ in (5mm) strip of vanilla bean

Otherwise known as parfait-amour, this sweet violet liqueur makes a delicious after-dinner drink. Its deep purple colour and heady aroma put it in a class of its own.

Put all the ingredients in a jar and leave for several weeks, shaking occasionally. When ready, strain through muslin, then again through a coffee filter paper, until clear. For an even prettier effect, you can add a few drops of purple food colouring. **Makes 1pt (600ml)**

FLORAL ICE CUBES

Suitable flowers include : rose petals, tiny sprigs of mint or thyme in flower, scented geranium blooms, primroses, violets, borage (Borago) and lavender.
Ice tray and water

Flowers or petals encapsulated in cubes of ice look wonderfully pretty floating in summer drinks or used as table decorations. Float them in bowls of wine cup or pile them around a glass serving dish filled with a cool, creamy, summer pudding.

Put a flower in each ice-tray section. Half fill with water and freeze. Top up with water and freeze again. Freezing like this means the flower is in the middle of the ice, as it tends to float to the top of the water.

BELOW: Rich, heady violet liqueur is not surprisingly known as 'perfect love'.

LEFT: Decorated with borage and fresh mint, this cooling claret cup is based on a 19th-century recipe.

BELOW: Edible flowers encased in ice make enchanting and unusual decorations for special summer drinks.

117

APPLE-MINT LEMONADE

4 lemons
3½ oz (100g / ½ cup) of caster
(superfine) sugar
1¼ pt (750ml / 2¾ cups) of water
Apple mint and/or lemon balm sprigs
Mint flowers and sprigs to decorate

Home-made lemonade is easy to make and this version has the refreshing taste of apple mint as a bonus. If you intend to store the lemonade for long, it's best to remove the lemon rind (zest) from the fruit first, as it can give the drink a bitter taste.

Scrub the lemons thoroughly to remove any wax or residual spray. Peel strips thin-

Home-made lemonade is enhanced by adding lemon balm or apple mint.

ly from the skin and put them into a heat-proof jug. Add the sugar and pour over just enough boiling water to dissolve it. Finally, add the sprigs of mint and leave to cool.

 118

Squeeze the juice from the lemons into the syrup. Remove the mint, but leave the lemon peel. Top up with cold water according to taste.

When ready to serve, add plenty of ice and slices of freshly cut lemon. Decorate with a couple of sprigs of fresh mint — flowering mint looks particularly attractive when in season.

ROSE AND VANILLA TEA BAGS

2 cups of dried scented rose petals
6 dried rose hips
Dried rind (zest) of 1 orange
1 vanilla pod
Nappy (diaper) liners
Cotton twist thread

The subtle combination of aromatic vanilla and scented rose makes a refreshing drink. You can either drink it hot or chilled for a sensational summer drink.

Carefully strip the peel off the rose hips and chop it up. Then add a finely chopped vanilla pod and the dried rind (zest) of the orange peel. Cut the rose petals into very small pieces and add to the mixture. Stir well with a metal spoon.

Cut each nappy (diaper) liner into four circles. Place two teaspoons of the mixture

BELOW: Rose and vanilla tea bags make a refreshing drink, either hot or cold.

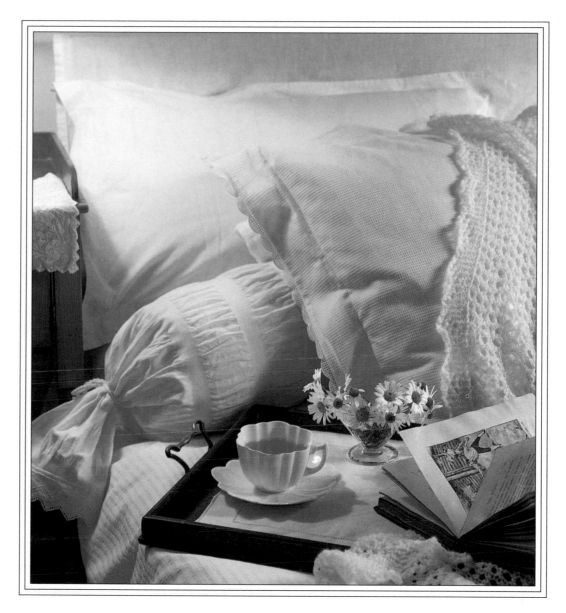

ABOVE: Chamomile tisane is easily made by infusing a spoonful of dried flowers in a teapot of boiling water. After a few minutes the tisane can be strained before drinking.

in the centre of each circle. Bring the edges to the centre and tie tightly with cotton twist, leaving one long end for ease of handling. Trim the surplus from the top of the liner, and store in an airtight tin.

When making the tea, allow one bag per cup. Pour boiling water on to the bag and leave to steep for five minutes. If desired, you can sweeten the tea with honey.

TISANES

As well as adding scent and flavour to conventional teas, flowers can be used to make tisanes. Use 1 teaspoon of dried flowers or 3 teaspoons of fresh per cup, and steep them in boiling water for about 3 or 4 minutes before drinking. Make in a jug and strain into a cup. Add a slice of lemon and sweeten with honey if desired.

You can also add flowers to ordinary loose tea by adding roughly 2 tablespoons of either strongly scented rose petals, jasmine, marigold or lime flowers to 6 tablespoons of tea leaves.

 119

FLOWERS FOR BEAUTY

Small muslin bags filled with flowers and herbs scent bath water in a natural way.

We never seem to grow tired of flower scents in the beauty preparations we use. And nowadays, more than ever before, we feel the need for simple and straightforward products that are as far removed as possible from the chemist's laboratory. This chapter is packed with ideas for making your own preparations from a wide range of pure, natural ingredients.

120

The rose has a long association with beauty. Its irresistible fragrance makes it a popular choice for perfuming all kinds of beauty products, from shampoo to hand cream.

There is a long tradition of using flowers for beauty. In addition to their usefulness as medicines, flowers, leaves and herbs were long ago discovered to have all kinds of therapeutic and beneficial qualities when they were steeped in various lotions and creams, or simply used as an infusion.

Throughout the centuries, flowers were found to contain qualities that soothed and softened skin, brightened and strengthened hair, or simply relaxed and scented a tired body in a deliciously fragrant bath.

There are many recipes that you can make at home. You could start with a simple infusion of flowers to use as a foot bath or facial, or try some scented bath bags.

The recipes in this chapter are made with pure, natural ingredients. Be aware, however, that the properties of some plants are stronger than others and, although it is extremely unlikely, there is the possibility that some ingredients may irritate sensitive skin. If you are sensitive to certain plants, you can always adapt and alter a recipe to suit your taste.

STERILIZING BOTTLES AND JARS

To keep all your recipes free from possible contamination, it is best to sterilize all the bottles or jars that you intend to use.

The oldest method of sterilization is to boil the item but today this is not the best method, particularly if you are using delicate glass. Instead, try one of the sterilizing products on the market, which are either for use with babies' feeding bottles or for home wine making. Simply follow the manufacturer's instructions.

REFRIGERATION

Many home-made creams and lotions benefit from being kept in the refrigerator. As the recipes involve natural products, they are unlikely to last as long as commercial preparations. Keeping them cold will not only preserve them longer, it will also help to improve the efficacy of some preparations — toners, for example, feel great when applied icy cold.

MAKING SACHETS

Bath sachets are easily made from muslin, cheesecloth or any gauzy fabric through which the ingredients can infuse.

They are nothing more than strips of fabric about 13in by 3in (33cm by 8cm) which are folded in half and sewn up both sides. Once they have been turned the right way and filled with the ingredients, the top edge can be pinked or neatly hemmed and tied with pretty ribbon or string.

If sewing doesn't appeal to you, you can make a bath bag very easily without having to pick up a needle. Simply cut a square or circle of fabric and put a spoonful of your chosen mixture in the middle. Gather up the edges and tie the sachet securely with string, ribbon or thread.

ROSE PETAL WATER

5 cups of fresh, strongly scented, rose petals
Bottled mineral water
Vodka or
pure medicinal alcohol

Home-made rose petal water is lovely to use as a mild skin toner and freshener. It is gentle and sweetly fragrant and you can

This lovely fragrant Rose Petal Water is ideal as a gentle, fragrant skin tonic.

also use it to sprinkle in your bath water.

Put the rose petals into a large bowl and heat up the mineral water. When the water has reached boiling point, pour it over the rose petals.

When cool, mix in the vodka. Do not buy good quality spirit — cheap vodka works just as well. You will need one part vodka to 10 parts water. Leave to infuse.

When cold, strain the rose-petal liquid into sterilized bottles. A petal or two added to the bottle before sealing adds a decorative touch. Cap the bottle securely with a cork or tight stopper.

ROSE LOTION

2 cups of deep red rose petals, fresh or dried
1 cup of bottled mineral water
1 cup of white wine vinegar
½ cup of bought rosewater

This is an alternative recipe to the Rose Petal Water that doesn't use alcohol.

Put the petals in a screw-top jar. Boil the water and vinegar and pour on the petals. Leave for several days, shaking it daily. Then, add the rosewater, shake well and decant into a sterilized, stoppered bottle.

POPPY AND CORNFLOWER LOTION

2 tbsp of dried poppy petals
1 tbsp of dried cornflowers
½ pt (300ml) of bottled mineral water

This recipe is a mild facial skin toner. If you keep it in the refrigerator it will feel especially invigorating and refreshing when you apply it to your skin.

BELOW: This alcohol-free Rose Lotion makes a wonderful skin tonic.

RIGHT: A mildly astringent toner, Poppy and Cornflower Lotion lasts well when kept in the refrigerator.

Put the poppy petals and cornflowers into a small saucepan and then add the bottled water. Bring the mixture to the boil and turn off the heat. Allow the petals to infuse for at least 30-40 minutes.

When the solution is ready and has completely cooled, strain it through a fine sieve into a jug. Finally, pour it into sterilized glass bottles and seal with a cork.

ROSE PETAL FACIAL STEAM

1¾ pt (1 litre) of bottled mineral water
5 tbsp of fresh, strongly scented rose petals
2-3 drops of rose essential oil

A facial steam is a wonderful relaxant and helps open up pores to rid the skin of blackheads and other horrors.

Heat the water to boiling. Put the petals in a large bowl and pour the water over them. Add the essential oil, stir well and leave to infuse for 3 minutes.

To use the facial steam, hold your face over the bowl, but make sure you don't get too close to the water as the skin on your face is very delicate and you could cause broken veins. Drape a towel over your head to enclose the steam. Try to remain over the steam for about 10 minutes if you can, but take a breather every now and then. Finish off by dousing your skin with lukewarm water and a splash of facial tonic such as rose petal water (see page 122).

Herbs, like peppermint, sage and rosemary can all be added to the water to give a more astringent facial.

ABOVE: Pretty pink Carnation and Clove Soaps welcome guests to the washroom. They also make ideal gifts.

ABOVE: Made with floral essential oils and pure soap, these Geranium Soap Balls are kind to most skin types.

LEFT: Pure luxury and ten minutes' enforced rest come with this sweetly scented Rose Petal Facial Steam.

GERANIUM SOAP BALLS

1 large bar of unscented white soap
2fl oz (55ml) of bought rosewater
2 drops of grapefruit essential oil
2 drops of rose geranium essential oil
Lemon food colouring (optional)

These scented guest soaps make a lovely gift when they are wrapped in cellophane and tied with a pretty posy of dried flowers or leaves.

First grate the soap into a bowl. Then gently heat the rosewater in a heatproof bowl over a pan of simmering water. Pour the rosewater over the grated soap and stir.

To this softened mixture carefully add the essential oils, drop by drop, and mix thoroughly with a metal spoon. If you want to colour the soap, now is the time to add the lemon food colouring. When the soap is well blended, let it stand for one or two days. Then break it into small pieces and roll each one into a ball.

Polish the soap balls with cotton wool (absorbent cotton) dipped in a little rosewater or almond oil.

CARNATION AND CLOVE SOAP

10oz (300g) of plain, unscented soap
9fl oz (250ml) of water
4 drops of pink food colouring
5 drops of carnation essential oil
1 drop of clove essential oil

A lovely gift idea, but you might prefer to keep these pretty soaps for yourself!

Grate the soap into a mixing bowl. Boil the water and pour it over the soap. Add the food colouring and stir well.

Take the essential oils and add them to the mixture, drop by drop. Mix the ingredients thoroughly with a metal spoon and leave the mixture to harden.

When the soap has hardened, break off small pieces and mould them into smallish balls. When they are really hard, polish each ball of soap with a little cotton wool (absorbent cotton) dipped into almond oil.

BATH BAG

1 cup of wheat bran
1 cup of oatmeal
½ cup of dried milk powder
1 cup of dried, highly scented rose petals
1 cup of dried lavender flowers
½ cup of dried lemon verbena leaves
or rosemary

These simple bath sachets can be hung from the running hot water tap or placed into the bath itself. The bran, oatmeal and milk act as water softeners. The other ingredients are for fragrance and can be adapted to suit personal preferences.

Mix all the ingredients together in a large bowl, then spoon the mixture into sachets (instructions for making these appear on page 121). Any surplus mixture can be stored in a screw-top jar.

ROSE GERANIUM BUBBLE BATH

5fl oz (150ml) of pure organic washing-up
(dish-washing) liquid
5fl oz (150ml) of still bottled mineral water
1 tsp of rose geranium essential oil
3 drops of pink food colouring

A fun and foaming bubble bath in a pretty pink makes a lovely gift either for yourself or for a friend.

In a small jug mix the washing-up liquid with the mineral water. Add the essential oil and stir well. To this solution add the food colouring and stir well once more.

Decant the mixture into a pretty bottle which can be decorated with some ribbon

BELOW: Bath bags may be dropped straight into the water or tied to a bath tap.

ABOVE: Rose Geranium Bubble Bath makes a lovely gift, but you can mix some just for yourself!

or a few silk flowers. Add one tablespoon of bubble bath to hot running water for a fragrant and luxurious bath.

ROSE BATH OIL

3 tbsp of glycerine
1 tbsp of rose essential oil

Bath oils help to make a relaxing experience even more pleasurable. The beauty of this bath oil is that it doesn't rely on artificial fragrances or colours, and it will help condition your skin as well.

Simply mix the glycerine well with the essential oil using a metal spoon.

Keep bottled and use only one teaspoon per bath, pouring it into the stream of running hot water.

RIGHT: A bath scented with roses is both luxurious and relaxing.

CHAMOMILE HAIR RINSE

*4 tbsp of fresh chamomile flowerheads or
2 tbsp of dried
18fl oz (500ml) of bottled mineral water
2 tbsp of distilled vinegar*

Hair rinses can be infused with many different herbs and flowers according to your hair type and colour.

Chamomile has long been used for its slight lightening qualities on blond hair, but for brown hair, substitute sage, rosemary or marigold for a darker sheen (see recipe for Rosemary and Lavender Hair Rinse below).

To make this rinse, first boil the water in a pan and add the chamomile. Take the pan off the heat and leave to infuse, then add the vinegar and allow to cool. Strain and store the mixture in sterilized bottles.

The hair rinse should be used after shampooing as follows: mix six tablespoons of rinse with 1 pint (500 ml) of warm water and pour over your hair. Towel dry and style your hair as usual.

ROSEMARY AND LAVENDER HAIR RINSE

*1 tbsp of dried lavender flowers
1 tbsp of dried rosemary
½ pt (300ml) of water
1pt (600ml) of bottled mineral water
1 tsp of lemon juice or good wine vinegar*

This rinse is excellent for dark hair. (For instructions on how to use, see recipe for Chamomile Hair Rinse above).

Pour the ordinary water into a saucepan and add the lavender flowers and rosemary. Gently bring the water to the boil. Take off the heat and allow to infuse for several hours. Strain off the liquid and add it to the bottled mineral water. Add the lemon juice or wine vinegar and pour the mixture into sterilized bottles.

*LEFT: Used regularly, Chamomile Hair Rinse
is said to lighten fair hair and add shine.*

ELDERBERRY HAIR RINSE

4oz (115g) of fresh elderberries
(Sambucus nigra)
1pt (½ litre) of water

This is a simple recipe for those with grey hair. Use it as a final rinse to impart a slight blue/grey tint to the hair.

Put the elderberries into a bowl and crush them slightly. Bring the water to the boil and pour it over the berries. Then stir the mixture and leave it to infuse for approximately two hours.

When ready, strain the liquid into a sterilized bottle. Use the rinse as instructed in the Chamomile Hair Rinse recipe on the previous page.

It is worth looking out for pretty bottles you can use to store rinses such as this. Flea markets and bric-a-brac stalls often sell old bottles quite cheaply.

An attractive assortment of pretty bottles holds a fragrant range of floral waters (see recipes on pages 122-123) and hair rinses.

ROSE HAND CREAM

2 tbsp of fresh rose petals
4 tbsp of almond oil
8 tbsp of lanolin
4 tbsp of glycerine
4 or 5 drops of rose essential oil

Use this soothing lotion to condition hands, feet or elbows.

First, cover the rose petals with a little boiling water and leave to cool. Then gently melt the almond oil, lanolin and glycerine in a bowl over a saucepan of hot water.

Put the almond oil mixture, well-drained rose petals and rose oil into a food processor and blend thoroughly.

Finally, pour the hand cream into small sterilized glass jars with tight-fitting lids.

LEFT: A rich Rose Hand Cream can easily be made from natural ingredients.

BELOW: A beautiful shade of lemony orange, this Orange and Carrot Moisturiser uses natural carrot juice and essential oil.

ORANGE AND CARROT MOISTURISER

1 tsp of beeswax
1 tbsp of lanolin
6 tbsp of almond oil
3 tbsp of bottled mineral water
4 tbsp of carrot juice
$\frac{1}{2}$ tsp of borax
2 tbsp of glycerine
3 drops of sweet orange essential oil

This scented moisturiser helps protect your skin from everyday wear and tear.

Melt the beeswax with the lanolin and almond oil in a bowl set over a saucepan of simmering water. Stir gently until the ingredients have melted.

In another small saucepan, heat the water and carrot juice and dissolve the borax.

Then add the glycerine to the beeswax mixture and stir well. Remove the bowl from the saucepan and slowly add the carrot juice mixture to the beeswax mixture, whisking thoroughly until the ingredients have cooled down.

Add the essential oil and mix well. Put into a clean jar with a tight fitting lid and store in a cool place or the refrigerator.

Orange Flower Night Cream is a nourishing blend of natural oils, wax and lanolin.

ORANGE FLOWER NIGHT CREAM

2 tsp of lanolin
2 tsp of beeswax
4 tsp of almond oil
3 tsp of bottled mineral water
Pinch of borax
4 capsules of wheatgerm oil
3 or 4 drops of neroli (orange blossom) essential oil

Scented with sweet orange blossom, this is a wonderfully rich and nourishing cream that is ideal for smoothing and softening dry skin overnight.

Put the lanolin, beeswax and almond oil into a heatproof bowl and stand it over a saucepan of simmering water. Gently stir the ingredients until they melt.

In another bowl, put the borax. Heat the bottled water in a separate pan and pour it over the borax. Stir well and add the lanolin mixture to it.

Pierce the wheatgerm capsules and stir these into the creamy mixture. Finally, add the essential oil and stir thoroughly with a metal spoon so that it is well distributed.

The cream should be put straight into a container with a tight-fitting lid before it begins to set. Store it in a cool place or the door of a refrigerator.

PEACH AND MARIGOLD FACE PACK

1 fresh peach
10 marigold flowerheads
Ground almonds

Marigolds have long been known for their soothing properties on skin irritated by fierce sun or wind. Here is a simple recipe for a fruity mask which will help to freshen and soften the whole face.

Pick the petals from each flowerhead and put them into a food processor. Then peel the peach and slice the flesh into small pieces. Add the peach to the petals and process them quickly. Finally, stir in enough ground almonds to make a thick paste. Apply the pack to clean skin, avoiding your

The healing properties of marigold petals have long been exploited. Here they combine with fresh peach and almonds to make a soothing, skin softening face mask.

eyes, and leave for 15 minutes before rinsing it off with warm water. Keep any extra face pack in the refrigerator.

ABOVE: *Dried marigold petals combine with natural yoghurt to make a therapeutic and uplifting face mask.*

Pour the oats into a mixing bowl. If you prefer to make a finer mask, you can process the oats in a food processor or blender for a few seconds first.

Add the rosewater to the oats, working the mixture into a paste. Watch the consistency — if the mask is too thin or too thick, it will simply slide off your face.

Finally, add 2 drops of rose essential oil and mix the paste thoroughly.

To use, apply the mask to the face, avoiding the areas close to your eyes, and leave for about 15 minutes. Rinse off with lukewarm water and pat your face dry. Finish with a mild toner to close up the pores.

MARIGOLD MASK

6 tbsp of dried marigold (any variety) petals
4 tbsp of good quality natural yoghurt
3 tbsp of bottled mineral water
4 tbsp of oatmeal
1 tbsp of wheatgerm

This mask is wonderfully restorative, but it must be applied while it is still warm, so it cannot really be stored.

Put the marigold petals into a bowl, heat the bottled water and pour it over the petals. Add the oatmeal and wheatgerm and stir vigorously. Pour in the yoghurt and continue to mix well.

Making sure the mask is warm but not too hot, apply it to your face, avoiding the eyes. It should be left on for 20-30 minutes and rinsed off with lukewarm water.

LEFT: *This mildly abrasive Rosewater and Oat Face Mask sloughs off dead cells to revitalize your skin.*

ROSEWATER AND OAT FACE MASK

3-4 tbsp of porridge oats
1-2 tbsp of rosewater
2 drops of rose essential oil

This natural face mask is a wonderful cleanser. It helps unclog pores and remove dead cells which make the skin look dull.

LEFT: *Put into an old-fashioned powder bowl, this lavender and herbal talc gives a luxurious finish to bath – or showertime.*

Bergamot Cologne is a delicious after-bath, splash-on cologne, with a fragrance that is suitable for men or women.

Take the rose and carnation, strip off all the petals and put them into a screw-top jar. Pour the vodka over the petals. Screw the top on to the jar, shake well and leave the mixture to stand on a sunny windowsill for about a week.

When the petals are ready, bring the bottled water to the boil. Put the orange peel and cloves into a bowl and pour the boiling water over them. Leave this mixture to stand for about 5-6 hours.

Strain both the petal/vodka mixture and the orange/clove mixture through a fine sieve into a glass jug. Check for clarity. You may find that the mixture needs straining again through a finer sieve or a coffee filter paper to clear it completely.

Finally, add the bergamot essential oil drop by drop and stir well. Decant the mixture into a sterilized bottle and keep in a cool place between use.

HERBAL TALCUM POWDER

*5 tbsp of lavender flowers or any other
perfumed flowers of your choice
2 tbsp of dried, chopped mixed herbs
10 tbsp unscented talcum powder
1 tbsp of lavender essential oil*

As a welcome change to ready-scented talcum powder, why not buy the unperfumed type and add your own scents?

This recipe uses lavender and herbs, but you could experiment using other kinds of fresh flowers such as roses or jasmine combined with their matching essential oils.

Put the lavender flowers (or the flowers of your choice) and the mixed herbs into a blender or food processor and process them to a fine powder. You will find that this is quite a lengthy process, but it needs to be done thoroughly.

First, sieve the talcum powder into a bowl and add the powdered lavender and herbs. Then add the essential oil carefully, mixing it in thoroughly before transferring the powder to an old-fashioned powder bowl or other shallow container with a lid.

BERGAMOT COLOGNE

*1 fresh, sweet-scented rose
1 scented carnation
4fl oz (115ml) of cheap vodka
3 tbsp of dried orange peel (zest)
1 tsp of cloves
$\frac{1}{2}$ pt (350ml) of bottled mineral water
3 drops of bergamot essential oil*

Infused with cloves, orange and petals, this Bergamot Cologne has a fresh fragrance, ideal for après bathtime.

ABOVE: Leafy Aftershave makes the ideal gift with its subtle fragrance and mildly astringent properties.

LEAFY AFTERSHAVE

3 tbsp of dried strawberry leaves
3½ fl oz (100ml) of bottled mineral water
4fl oz (115ml) of rosewater
1 tsp of borax

A fine gift for the men in your life, this subtle, leafy splash-on is best kept stored in the refrigerator.

Put the strawberry leaves into a heatproof bowl. In a small saucepan, bring the bottled mineral water to the boil and pour over the strawberry leaves. Let this solution infuse for about 4–5 hours.

Then pour the rosewater into another heatproof bowl. Set this over a saucepan of simmering water and heat the rosewater through. When it's hot, add the borax, stirring very gently until all the borax has dissolved. Remove from the heat.

To the rosewater and borax mixture add the strawberry leaf solution, straining it first through a fine sieve in order to remove all traces of the leaves.

Finally, pour the aftershave into an attractive, sterilized bottle.

LAVENDER AND MINT FOOT BATH

3½ pt (2 litres) of bottled mineral water
3 stems of fresh peppermint or 1 tbsp of dried
6 stems of fresh lavender or 2 tbsp of dried
1 or 2 drops of lavender essential oil

Using fragrant lavender and mint flowers, this foot bath is a quick, effective pick-me-up for tired, aching feet. If you prefer, you could try using rosemary as a refreshing alternative to lavender.

First, heat 10fl oz (300ml) of mineral water to boiling point and pour this over the flowers in a small bowl or jug. Leave the mixture to infuse for at least 15 minutes, then strain into a large bowl.

Add the oil, stir well and top up with the rest of the warm water .

BELOW: A lavender and peppermint foot bath, here infusing before use, is a wonderful refresher for aching feet.

FLORAL GIFTS

*A range of pretty stationery can be easily
scented to make a most welcome gift.*

In this chapter you will find ways of using dried
flowers, pressed flowers and pot-pourri to make a
selection of lovely gifts. From simple scented
sachets and notepaper to more complex wardrobe
sets, there's something for everyone to
enjoy making and giving.

This notepaper and envelope set has been stored with lavender bundles to give it a distinctive fragrance.

M ost of the gift ideas on the following pages use materials that are readily available, such as scraps of fabric and ribbon, little boxes or stationery. By adding a few dried flowers, some home-made pot-pourri or a pretty pressed-flower design, you have an individual and highly personalized gift which will delight anyone.

LAVENDER SCENTED PAPER

Dried lavender flowerheads
1 tsp of orris root powder
2 or 3 drops of lavender essential oil
Lavender coloured notepaper and envelopes
Net
Ribbon or fine wire

Perfume readily available stationery with a matching fragrance for a delightful gift. The notepaper and envelopes are simply stored together with a strong pot-pourri which imparts its fragrance to the paper.

First make the pot-pourri. Mix the dried lavender together with the orris root and the essential oil, stirring well with a metal spoon until all the oil has been well dispersed among the flowers.

Make little sachets by cutting out several circles of net. Fill each one with the pot-pourri and secure tightly with a ribbon or piece of wire. Place these net bundles into a box containing the stationery and leave for at least one week, longer if possible, before repackaging the gift.

Stick a few stems of lavender on to the lid of the box for a finishing touch.

TEDDY PINCUSHION

Pot-pourri (see recipes on pages 88-97)
10in (25cm) circle of lace fabric
8in (20cm) circle of cotton fabric
Scraps of lace and ribbon
Polyester wadding
Needle and thread
Small toy teddy or doll

This little teddy makes a charming gift and can be used simply for decoration if not as a pincushion.

Line the lace fabric with the cotton, neatly stitching the two together. Then sew running stitch around the edge of the lace circle, leaving the end of the thread loose for gathering later. Lay the circle lace side down, and put some wadding on top. Thenplace the teddy in the centre of the wadding and add the pot-pourri.

Pull the running stitch tight to gather up the lace circle around the teddy's waist, and fasten off firmly. Make two shoulder

BELOW: This little teddy's skirt emits a lovely fragrance and makes a practical pincushion as well as a cute decoration.

straps from ribbon or lace, securing them with a couple of stitches. Finally, decorate the cushion with lace gathered around the teddy's waist, finishing off with a bow.

SWEET BAG

For the sweet bag mixture:
1 cup of strongly scented dried rose petals
1 cup of dried lavender
½ cup of dried lemon verbena leaves
½ cup of crushed dried rosemary
2 tbsp of orris root powder
2 crushed cinnamon sticks
3 drops of rose essential oil

For the bag:
Fine, lace edged, cotton lawn handkerchief
Bright check ribbon

ABOVE: For quick results, make a pretty sweet bag from a lacy handkerchief.

A sweet bag is an old-fashioned term for a scented drawer or linen sachet. The one shown here is the simplest of all to make, requiring no sewing. Use the recipe here for the filling, or choose any of the other pot-pourri recipes on pages 88-97.

Make the filling by mixing together all the dry ingredients in a large bowl using a metal spoon. Add the essential oil, and stir well. Put the mixture in a sealed container, give it a shake, then leave it in a dark place for about four weeks.

When the mixture is ready, pour it into the centre of the lace handkerchief. Gather the handkerchief up around the pot-pourri and tie it firmly with ribbon.

ADDRESS BOOK

Pressed white larkspur buds and leaves
Plain black address book
Tweezers
Latex adhesive
Self-adhesive protective film

Enhance a plain black address book with a column of pressed white flowers to make an attractive gift.

First, place the largest larkspur bud at the bottom edge of the book, about ½ in (1cm) in from both edges. Fix with a dab of adhesive. With the aid of the tweezers, gently position the flowers up the book, using buds of decreasing size, and angling them to give interest. Secure each one with a little adhesive.

When the design is complete, seal it with a strip of protective film. The film should measure the height of the book, plus a 1in (2.5cm) overlap, and the width of the design, plus ½ in (1cm). Finally, rub the film down carefully, turning in the overlap on all three sides.

BELOW: Dress up a black address book by decorating it with pressed larkspur flowers.

This scented hot water bottle cover has a sachet tucked into its appliquéd pocket.

FRAGRANT HOT WATER BOTTLE

Quilted floral fabric and lining fabric
Other scraps of fabric
Contrasting sewing thread
Satin ribbon
Herbal pot-pourri (for recipes see pages 88-97)

Herbs and flowers are often used to relax and soothe. The heat from the bottle will help release the soothing fragrance.

Draw around the hot water bottle to make a template and use this to cut out two pieces of quilted fabric and two of lining, allowing extra for a seam allowance.

From the fabric scraps, cut out three or four flower shapes. Using machine zig-zag stitch, appliqué these to one of the quilted bottle shapes. From another fabric scrap, cut a basket shape and handle. Sew these in front of the flowers as shown, leaving the top of the basket open to form a pocket.

Stitch the lining to the right side of the quilted fabric, leaving a gap, and turn out. Repeat to make the back of the cover, then hand-stitch the gaps closed. Then with right sides together, stitch both the bottle shapes together, leaving an opening at the 'shoulders' of the bottle.

For the sachet, cut out two more flower shapes and, wrong sides together, machine zig-zag around the edges, leaving a small gap to fill the sachet with pot-pourri. Stitch up the opening. Tuck this flower sachet into the 'basket' and, to finish, add a little bow to the opening at the top of the bottle.

PERFUME POCKET

Pot-pourri (for recipes, see pages 88-97)
Small cushion and cover made
with floral fabric
Scrap of fabric to match or complement
the cushion cover
Narrow satin ribbon
Needle and thread
Pins

A pretty floral cushion, complete with a pocket and scented sachet, makes a superb gift. You can either make your own cushion cover, or buy one and team up a scrap of fabric to make the pocket and sachet.

Cut a rectangle from the scrap of fabric to sit on the front of the cushion. As a general guide, if your cushion measures 12in (30cm) square, the pocket should measure about 3in by 4in (7.5cm by 10cm). Turn under one long edge and hem. Turn under the other three sides and press. Pin the rectangle to the front of the cushion cover, while keeping the hemmed edge at the top. Neatly stitch the pocket to the cover.

To make the sachet, cut a long rectangle of fabric. (To fit the pocket measurements

A scented sachet is kept in a pocket sewn to one side of this pretty cushion.

above, the rectangle will need to be 10in by 3in (25cm by 7.5cm).) With wrong sides together, fold the rectangle in half and stitch up both long sides. Turn right sides out and hem around the top edge.

Fill the sachet with your chosen pot-pourri and tie the sachet with the ribbon. Tuck it into the cushion pocket to complete.

You can easily renew the pot-pourri if it loses its fragrance.

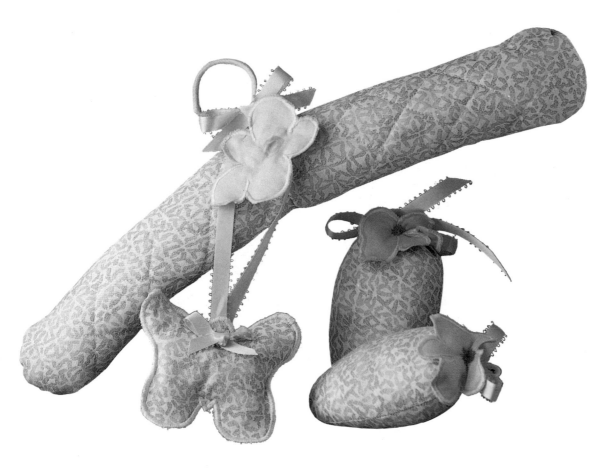

FRAGRANT WARDROBE SET

For the pot-pourri:
1 cup of dried lavender
1 cup of dried crumbled southernwood
½ cup of dried crumbled rosemary
2 crushed cinnamon sticks
Other materials:
Plain coat hanger
Floral fabric
Contrasting thread
Narrow ribbon to match the thread
Fabric scrap the same colour as the thread
Wadding and polyester stuffing

If you are handy with a needle and thread, you will enjoy making this pretty matching wardrobe set which consists of a scented hanger, sachet and shoe shapes.

First make the pot-pourri by combining all the ingredients. It is not necessary to leave this mixture to cure.

To make the hanger, mix the pot-pourri with some stuffing and wrap this around the hanger. Secure the scented stuffing to

ABOVE: A Fragrant Wardrobe Set makes a charming gift. It consists of a scented hanger, sachet and shoe shapes.

the hanger by winding thread around and around it. Line a piece of floral fabric with fine wadding and machine quilt. Use this to cover the hanger. Add a little satin bow by the hook.

For the sachet, cut out two butterfly shapes from the floral fabric and, with wrong sides together, machine zig-zag the edges. Leave a little gap and fill with pot-pourri and a little stuffing. Stitch up the gap and add a tiny ribbon bow to the front and a hanging ribbon loop.

The shoe shapes are made from oval-shaped pieces of floral fabric. Make sure that the shapes will comfortably fit inside your shoes.

Stitch two pieces of the fabric, right sides together, leaving a small gap to turn the shape right sides out. Pack the shape with stuffing and pot-pourri before stitching up

the opening. Add a satin ribbon bow to the top as a finishing touch.

The hanger and shoe shapes also have little fabric flowers stitched on to them. To make one flower, cut two flower shapes from the contrast fabric, place them wrong sides together and machine zig-zag around the edges. Add a little decorative stitch to the centre to finish.

INSECT DETERRENT

3 cups of dried santolina or
cotton lavender
1 tbsp of cloves
1 tbsp of caraway seeds
1 tbsp of mace
3 cinnamon sticks
Calico
String or twine

This makes a really useful present, especially during a hot summer! And it's so easy to create. Simply crush the cinnamon sticks in a bowl and mix with the other dry ingredients. Cut out several 10in (25cm) circles of calico and fill each one with a tablespoon of the spicy mixture. To complete, gather up the sides and tie with string.

BELOW: This is an unusual, but most useful, gift. These little bags contain a practical Insect Deterrent.

BERGAMOT AND ORANGE SACHET

Dried orange peel (zest)
Dried hebe leaves
2 tsp of orris root powder
2-3 drops of bergamot essential oil
10in (25cm) circle of lace fabric
1⅛ yd (l metre) of pre-gathered edging lace
1yd (90cm) of narrow peach
coloured ribbon
Needle and thread

This frothy boudoir sachet emits a lovely fragrance, and is really too pretty to tuck away in a drawer. Hang it in the wardrobe or from the mirror of a dressing table. Begin by making the pot-pourri. In a large bowl, mix together the orange peel, leaves, orris root powder and the bergamot oil. Stir well with a metal spoon. For a longer lasting scent, leave this mixture to mature in a sealed container for about a month, shaking it occasionally.

For the sachet, stitch the edging lace to the circle then thread the narrow ribbon through the lace, about 1in (2.5cm) in from the edge. Next, pull the ribbon to gather the edges of the lace into a bag shape. Fill the sachet with pot-pourri, gather the ribbon tightly and secure with a pretty bow.

BELOW: This lacy bundle emits a warm scent of bergamot and orange.

ABOVE: Choose a favourite special fragrance to make this pretty Perfume Pot.

PERFUME POT

Pressed flowers and leaves; used here are variegated geranium leaves, silverweed, yellow medick and wood avens
Small ceramic pot with lid that dismantles
3 tsp of shredded beeswax
2 tsp of almond oil
15 drops of concentrated essential oil of your choice
Drop of sap-green dye
Latex adhesive

This solid perfume is simple to make and looks so pretty in a matching ceramic jar—a perfect complement to any dressing table.

Begin by creating the floral design on the insert card supplied with the lid. Fix the foliage in place first with the adhesive to create a triangular shape (see pages 73-85 for more details). Follow this outline with the other flowers. Here, the bold flower-heads of the wood avens have been used as the focal point of the display.

To make the perfume, melt the wax and almond oil in a saucepan over a very low heat. Remove the pan and, when the mixture has cooled a little, add the perfume oil and dye and pour it into the trinket pot. It will then set hard and be ready for use.

LACE-TRIMMED SACHET

For the pot-pourri:
l cup of dried rose petals
l cup of dried lavender
½ cup of dried crushed rosemary
2 crushed sticks of cinnamon
2 tbsp of orris root powder
3 drops of rose essential oil

These feminine lace-trimmed sachets make perfect dressing table accessories.

For the sachet:
Two 5in (13cm) circles of fine cotton lawn
20in (50cm) of cotton lace
Ribbon rose
Narrow satin ribbon
Matching thread and needle

These exquisite lace-trimmed sachets are designed for scenting dressing table drawers and they make lovely gifts for female friends or relatives.

First make the pot-pourri by mixing all the dry ingredients in a large bowl. Add the essential oil and mix thoroughly. Put the mixture into a sealed container, shake well, and leave for about four weeks. (For other pot-pourri recipes see pages 86-97.)

To make the sachet, place the cotton circles, right sides together, and stitch around the edge, leaving a small gap. Turn the sachet right side out and press. Fill with the pot-pourri, taking care not to over-stuff the sachet and make it too bulky. Sew up the opening. Now add the lace edging, stitching it on neatly by hand. Finally, stitch on the ribbon rose and narrow ribbon.

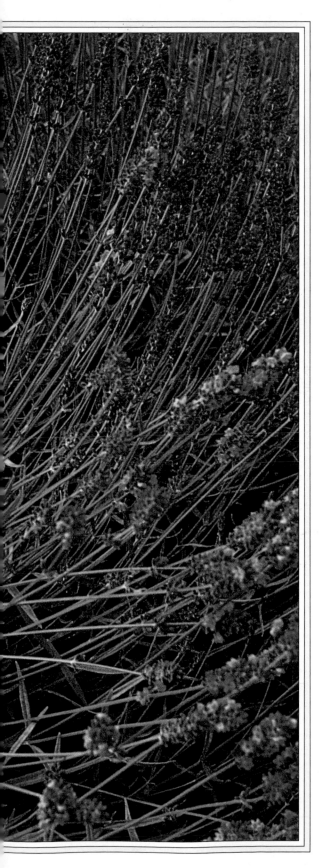

LAVENDER BOTTLES

Long stems of fresh lavender
Narrow lavender coloured ribbon or string

Lavender bottles are a charming and old-fashioned way of keeping clothes fresh and sweet smelling. Package some in a pretty basket as a delightful gift idea.

The method used to make the bottles is quite simple but you may need a little practice. Gather together a bunch of the lavender and tie a narrow piece of ribbon directly under the lavender heads.

Gently bend each stem back separately to encase the lavender heads and make a small cage. Tie another length of ribbon around the stems. Leave a loop of ribbon hanging so the lavender can dry naturally.

*LEFT: These old-fashioned Lavender Bottles
are an excellent way of keeping linen and
clothes fresh and sweet smelling.*

*ABOVE: Treat someone to a tried and tested
remedy for fine wooden furniture
with a pot of this fragrant Lavender
Furniture Polish.*

LAVENDER FURNITURE POLISH

$\frac{2}{3}$ cup of turpentine
$\frac{2}{3}$ cup of linseed oil
$\frac{1}{3}$ cup of cider vinegar
$\frac{1}{3}$ cup of methylated spirits
10 drops of lavender essential oil
Screw-top jar and gift jar

This beautifully fragrant polish makes an unusual but welcome gift to lovers of fine wooden furniture. The polish feeds wood and buffs to a really good shine.

Pour all the ingredients into the screw-top jar, screw the lid on tightly and shake really thoroughly. When mixed, pour into the gift jar and secure the cork. Finally, add a gift tag listing the ingredients and a note explaining the nature of the contents.

POSY BOXES

Dried, small-headed flowers such as
larkspur, sunray, small roses, golden rod,
amaranthus, gypsophila (baby's breath)
Fine florists' wire
Satin or gift ribbon
All-purpose glue

A delicate posy of dried flowers provides a perfect decoration for any gift. It can also be detached from the present and kept as an additional memento. Match the flowers to the giftwrap by choosing complementary colours. Alternatively, you could use plain giftwrap and any floral combination.

Gather a selection of dried flowers together and arrange them into an attractive shape. Bind the stems together firmly with wire. Now wrap ribbon around the stems to cover the wire and finish off with a bow. Attach the posy to the gift with glue.

GILDED BAY LEAVES

Nuts and whole dried bay leaves
Gold giftwrap
Wide ribbon and gold cord
Metallic paint in two or three colours
Hot glue gun or all-purpose glue

Create a really special present by decorating
your gift with golden bay leaves.

Dried flowers and leaves give a wrapped present an extra special finishing touch.

First, paint the bay leaves on both sides with the metallic paint. Use bronze, copper and gold paints for a range of different finishes. Leave the leaves to dry completely on a wire cooling rack used for baking.

Wrap the gift with gold paper and tie it with wide giftwrap or satin ribbon, finishing with a generous bow. Tuck the gold cord into this ribbon bow and then tie the gold cord in a little bow. For speedy results, use a hot glue gun to stick the gilded leaves to the ribbon. Stick on a few nuts as well.

FLOWERY GIFT BOXES

A selection of small boxes
Magazine and seed catalogue cut-outs
Floral wallpaper or giftwrap
All-purpose glue or double-sided tape
Clear varnish
Dried flowers (optional)

ABOVE: Make a selection of Posy Boxes for
extra-special gift wrapped presents.

RIGHT: This simple circular box filled with
pot-pourri has been covered with a selection
of colourful flower pictures. Each one over-
laps the other to give a dense and rich effect.

Small boxes are ideal for gifts and they can be decorated in a number of ways.

Try covering a box with cut-outs from magazines and seed catalogues to create a pretty floral surface. Overlap the pictures to give a solid mass of colour. This technique is known as découpage. Always coat the finished box with clear varnish to seal the pictures. A simpler method is to cover a box with a piece of good quality floral wallpaper or giftwrap. Either coat the wrong side of the paper with adhesive and glue it to the box, or use double-sided tape.

If you wish, you can finish off with a spray of dried flowers on the box lid.

FLOWER CARE

Garden flowers are best cut in the early morning or evening, when transpiration is at its lowest. On a hot, sunny afternoon, they will naturally have less moisture in their cells and therefore be more prone to wilt.

As flowers always benefit from a long drink before they are used, this may determine just when they are gathered. Ideally, a drink overnight is perfect if they are to be used the next morning, so evening picking is probably best.

Always gather flowers quickly and put them into water as soon as possible. Choose fresh, healthy blooms just coming into full flower, or in slightly open bud.

Some flowers naturally last longer than others, but all can be prolonged with care. Condition the flowers as described below.

BUYING FLOWERS

Shop-bought flowers are usually conditioned before they are sold, but you can still re-cut the stems under water yourself. Once trimmed, give the flowers a long drink for a few hours before transferring them to shallow water and a warm room.

In the spring and summer there generally will be more choice of flowers available. The flowers are also likely to be less expensive than in the winter, when most of the florist's stock will either have been imported or grown in hot-house conditions.

Make sure you buy flowers from a shop or stall that has a quick turnover and fresh supplies brought in from markets at least twice a week.

Whenever you buy flowers, remember the golden rule is to look for good, crisp foliage, strong, straight stems and tight, firm flower buds.

CONDITIONING FLOWERS

1 Cut flower stems at a sharp angle, so that the maximum area of the cut end is exposed to the water. Do this under water if possible.

2 Peel back a little of the bark of woody stems of shrubs and trees, then hammer or split the first inch or so to allow the water to penetrate easily. This can be done with a hammer, sharp garden secateurs or strong scissors.

3 Stand the prepared flowers in a bucket filled with warm water and leave them to have a long drink for several hours or overnight. If the stems are bent and you want to straighten them, wrap the flowers tightly in newspaper and plunge into water. This method is effective for flowers such as tulips and gerbera.

4 Certain flowers exude a milky sap which interferes with their water intake. The stems of flowers such as poppies, euphorbia and ferns can be sealed by singeing the ends over a flame.

5 *The large, hollow stems of flowers such as delphiniums and amaryllis (Hippeastrum) can be filled with water and then plugged with a small piece of cotton wool. Stand the stems in water straight after this treatment.*

7 *Roses should have all their thorns removed, as well as any extra leaves and small branches. Strip the thorns off the stems with the blade of a pair of scissors, or use a tool available specially for this purpose.*

9 *If flowers wilt unexpectedly, try reviving them by recutting the stems and standing them in shallow hot water for about half an hour. Position the flowers away from the steam when adding the water.*

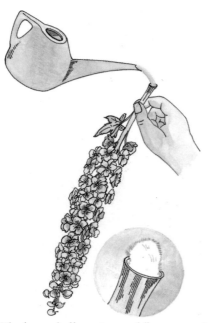

6 *Always strip the lower leaves off stems so that they do not sit under water in the vase. Rotting leaves will pollute the water and encourage the creation of bacteria, cloudy water and an unpleasant smell.*

8 *Some lilies have pollen-laden stamens that can brush against clothes and furnishings and stain indelibly. To prevent this from happening, carefully snip out the stamens using a little pair of manicure scissors.*

10 *Remove the topmost buds of flowers such as gladioli to ensure that the lower buds open. Condition foliage by immersing it in water for a few hours. Do not do this on grey- or silver-leaved foliage, or on plants with woolly foliage.*

TOOLS AND EQUIPMENT

CUTTING TOOLS

Essential tools for flower arranging are a pair of good-quality secateurs or florists' scissors with short blades. Also useful are scissors with a special wire-cutting notch.

WATERING EQUIPMENT

A long-spouted watering can is useful for reaching into large arrangements to top them up with clean water. Many flowers enjoy a fine hazy mist of water, so include a spray mister among your equipment.

TAPE

For posies and bouquets you may need the special tape for binding stems and wrapping around wires. Often known as gutta-percha tape, it comes in green, white and brown. Florists' adhesive tape is also available for sticking foam shapes together.

FLORISTS' FOAM

Blocks of wet foam for supporting fresh flowers in shallow containers are indispensable, as are blocks of the special type of foam available for dried flower arrangements. Both types of foam can be cut to any shape and size, and can easily be concealed, if necessary, with a layer of moss.

Most of the wet foam available today can be soaked in a minute or so. Allow the foam to stand above the edge of your container if you wish to add extra height to the flowers. Tape or wire the foam in position if necessary, or push it down on to a special florists' spike anchored with adhesive clay to the bottom of the container.

Foam does not look good in glass containers unless it is covered or hidden in some way, so save these for simple and informal arrangements.

WIRE

Different kinds of wire are useful. Stiff stub wire is excellent for dried flower displays, and a reel of fine rose wire is handy for many jobs. Wire mesh can be used as a support for large and heavy stems in a vase.

If cut at an angle, most stems will push easily into damp foam and will stay firmly put. However, if you are using plants with very soft stems you may need to spike holes first in the foam, into which the stems can then be inserted.

Flowers take up a lot of water, so remember to keep the foam damp by topping up the container with fresh water occasionally, particularly in warm conditions.

SUPPORTS FOR PLANTS

FUNNELS

If you are planning a really grand, large-scale arrangement for a special occasion, long funnels will be useful for adding extra height to individual flower stems.

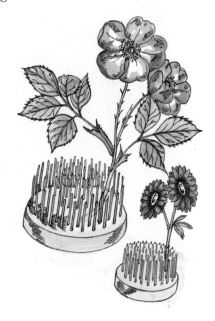

PINHOLDERS

Pinholders are heavy, metal blocks with sharp spikes and are a good way of securing some arrangements. Attach them to the base of the container with florists' putty, then insert the flowers among the spikes.

WIRE MESH

Crumpled wire mesh is very useful for supporting plants in wide-necked vases and shallow bowls, particularly if you are using large, woody-stemmed branches and top-heavy flowers. It can be jammed in place, or wired or taped inside the container.

MARBLES

Clear glass marbles make a pretty addition to a glass vase and they help hold stems in position. Clean, scrubbed pebbles can also be used for the same purpose.

TWIGS

To secure stems in exactly the right position in a container, cut a twig into small pieces and use these as a wedge or prop.

PROLONGING THE LIFE OF AN ARRANGEMENT

If your flowers have been conditioned well and are arranged in damp foam or water, they should last for a week or more depending on the variety. To help them last longer, always remember to keep the parts of the stems that are under water free from leaves, and use slightly warm water, never icy cold. Add a drop or two of bleach and a teaspoon of sugar to the water, or use the special crystals often provided by florists with cut flowers which help to prolong flower life. Replace the water after a few days if it is getting stale and remove and discard any plant material that is obviously tired, fading or dead. Cut out spent blooms and leave the buds to open out.

$\mathcal{F}$LOWERS TO GROW

Growing your own flowers is a very satisfying and absorbing hobby. It also makes gathering flowers and foliage for the projects in this book a lot less expensive. A garden is not vital to grow many varieties. Patios with pots and troughs, window boxes or small courtyards can all yield a wealth of material.

The following chart is a guide to growing your own plants. It has been divided into four major categories: fresh, dried, pressed and edible flowers. Many flowers can successfully be used in all these categories – roses, for example, are extremely versatile. Generally, each section gives a list of suitable plants, a brief description, and the best environment for growing them. It also gives the natural flowering seasons. The plants are listed alphabetically by Latin name. If you have trouble finding a plant and know it by its common name, look at the Scientific Classification chart on page 166.

RIGHT: *A well-planned border is not only decorative, it can provide a wealth of material for the projects and recipes featured in this book.*

FRESH FLOWERS			
NAME	TYPE/DESCRIPTION	CULTIVATION/ FLOWERING SEASON	CONDITIONING WHEN CUT
Alchemilla mollis Lady's mantle	Sprays of green-yellow flowers on saucer-shaped leaves. Very hardy herbaceous perennial.	Moist, well-drained soil in sun or partial shade. Flowers early summer.	Cut stems when the flowers are just starting to open. Split ends and give long, cool drink in deep water.
Alstroemeria sp. Peruvian lily	Azalea/lily-like flowers. Moderately hardy perennial.	Rich, well-drained soil in sun. Blooms late spring/early summer.	Cut stems, place in shallow water.
Anemone coronaria Florists' anemone	Bold coloured, bowl-shaped flowers with black central boss. Generally hardy.	Moist, well-drained humus-rich soil in sun or light shade. Plant late summer. Blooms spring.	Cut and dip stems in boiling water for a few seconds, then give long drink.
Aster sp. Aster	Daisy flowers usually pink, lavender or white. Herbaceous perennial.	Moist, fertile, well-drained soil in sun. Flowers late summer/ autumn.	Crush stem ends, place in boiling water then give overnight drink.
Centaurea cyanus Cornflower	Usually bright blue, also pink, purple, red and white. Annual.	Easy to grow border plants. Blooms summer.	Cut stems, place in water.

FRESH FLOWERS			
NAME	TYPE/DESCRIPTION	CULTIVATION/ FLOWERING SEASON	CONDITIONING WHEN CUT
Chrysanthemum sp. Chrysanthemum	Huge range of hybrids from pompon to daisies. Tender perennial.	Moist, well-drained fertile soil. Open position. Plant late spring. Blooms late summer/autumn.	Crush stem ends then give deep, cool drink.
Delphinium sp. Delphinium	Tall, usually blue, with spikes of flowers. Herbaceous perennial.	Prefers alkaline soil. Dislikes extreme summer heat. Blooms in summer.	Cut stems, turn upside down, fill stems with water and plug.
Dianthus sp. Carnations/pinks	Grass-like leaves. Single or double flowers often frilled. Pink, red, purple, white and yellow. Perennial – replace every few years.	Well-drained neutral or alkaline soil in full sun. Sow in spring from seed; cuttings in summer. Flowers in summer.	Cut stems at angle between joints and place in shallow, tepid water.
Freesia sp. Freesia	One-sided, arching spikes of waxy, funnel-shaped flowers with strong scent. White, pink, yellow, red, orange and purple. Tender, semi-hardy corm.	Well-drained soil in full sun. Plant outdoors in spring. Flowers late summer.	Cut stems, place in shallow water.
Gerbera Transvaal daisy	Brilliant coloured single or semi-single daisy. Semi-hardy perennial.	Moist, well-drained soil. Flowers early – mid-summer.	Cut stems on slant, put in boiling water for a few seconds. Give long, cool drink.
Gladiolus sp. Sword lilies	Tall, one-sided spikes of outward-facing, trumpet-shape flowers in wide colour range. Semi-hardy corms.	Well-drained soil in sun. Plant mid – late spring in batches, every two weeks. Flowers in summer.	Cut stems, put in cool, shallow water. Remove end buds for all flowers to open.
Gypsophila paniculata Baby's breath/ chalk plant	Profuse, tiny, white single flowers. Hardy perennial.	Well-drained, alkaline soil in sun. Blooms early – mid-summer.	Needs little conditioning except stem ends re-cut.

FRESH FLOWERS

Name	Type/description	Cultivation/ Flowering season	Conditioning when cut
Iris sp. Flag	Ruffled flowers on tall stems with lower petals ('falls'). Many colours, usually blue-purple and yellow. Very hardy evergreen rhizome. Also herbaceous *Iris* grown from bulb. More slender and delicate.	Moist, neutral/ lime-free soil in full sun. Blooms spring and early summer. Light, well-drained soil in full sun and shelter. Plant early autumn. Blooms late winter/spring.	Cut stems on slant, give long drink. As above.
Lilium sp. Lily	Most colours except blue. Trumpet-shaped, stately flowers. Very hardy bulb.	Well-drained soil in sun/partial shade. Plant autumn/early spring. Flowers early summer.	Cut stems on slant and give drink in cold water.
Moluccella laevis Bells of Ireland	Distinctive, tall, all-green plant. Half-hardy annual.	Light, rich, well-drained soil in full sun. Flowers summer.	Strip off most foliage. Put stems in ½ in of boiling water for 2 mins. Then give long cool drink.
Myosotis sylvatica Forget-me-not	Usually blue with white eye, also pink. Moderately hardy and grown as a biennial.	Fertile soil, generally sun. Blooms spring and early summer.	Cut stems, give long drink.
Narcissus sp. Daffodil/narcissus	Yellow, orange or white trumpet-shaped flower with outer petals. Very hardy perennial.	Well-drained soil in sun or partial shade. Plant bulbs late summer/early autumn. Blooms in spring.	Cut stems, put in cool, shallow water. Keep apart from other flowers for 24 hours as stems produce poison which kills other plants.

	FRESH FLOWERS		
NAME	TYPE/DESCRIPTION	CULTIVATION/ FLOWERING SEASON	CONDITIONING WHEN CUT
Paeonia sp. Peony	Red, white or pink, multi-petalled. Very hardy perennial.	Rich, well-drained soil in sun. Blooms early – mid-summer.	Cut ends, give long drink of warm water.
Ranunculus asiaticus Persian buttercup	Plump, cup-shaped, multi-petalled flowers in yellow orange, pink, red and white. Moderately hardy tuber.	Very good drainage, full sun. Plant early spring. Flowers late spring/ summer.	Cut ends, dip in boiling water, then give long drink.
Rosa sp. Rose	Wide variety of roses for easy growing in virtually every colour and shape. Grown as bushes, standards or climbers.	Well-drained soil with sun for several hours a day. Blooms generally in summer.	Crush ends with hammer, place in boiling water then give long drink. Can be revived with teaspoon of sugar.
Scabiosa sp. Scabious/ Pincushion flower	Daisy-like flowers with overlapping petals. Usually mauve-blue, also pink and white. Ultra-hardy perennial.	Likes sun. May need support. Flowers in summer.	Cut stems and give overnight drink.
Tulipa sp. Tulip	Bold colours, cup/goblet-shaped, six-petalled, single flowers. Also double varieties. Very hardy bulb.	Rich, well-drained soil in sun. Plant bulb mid autumn/early winter. Lift bulb when foliage dies, store till autumn. Blooms in spring.	Cut stems, wrap flowers in stiff paper for two hours. Place in shallow water.

DRIED FLOWERS			
NAME	TYPE/DESCRIPTION	CULTIVATION/ FLOWERING SEASON	METHOD OF PRESERVATION
Achillea sp. Yarrow	Flattish clusters of yellow flowers. Very hardy perennial.	Well-drained soil in full sun. Flowers early – late summer.	Air
Allium sp. Ornamental onion/ ornamental garlic	Small flowers in spheres. Usually blue or pink. Very hardy.	Easy in any well- drained, even poor, soil in sun or partial shade. Flowers early – mid-summer.	Air. Hang upside down until nearly dry. Then stand in tall container so that flowerhead regains shape.
Amaranthus caudatus Loves-lies-bleeding	Erect or drooping tassel-like flowers. Crimson or green. Half-hardy annual.	Any ordinary soil in sun. Flowers in summer.	Air
Anaphalis sp. Pearl everlasting	Silver- or grey- leaved plant with yellow-eyed white flowers in bunched heads. Hardy perennial.	Light, well- drained soil in sun. Flowers mid – late summer.	Air
Carthamus tinctorius Safflower	Thistle-like flowers in deep orange-yellow. Hardy annual.	Ordinary well- drained soil in full sun. Flowers mid-summer.	Air
Cynara scolymus Globe artichoke	Fat, thistle-like vegetable which dries beautifully Moderately hardy.	Well-drained soil in sun. Flowers mid-summer.	Air. Push short stems through wire mesh to support heads while drying.
Delphinium sp. Delphinium	see Fresh Flowers	see Fresh Flowers	Desiccant
Dipsacus sativus *(Dipsacus fullonum)* Teasel	Lavender coloured flowers which turn into heads of hooked prickles. Hardy biennial.	Rich, moist soil in sun or partial shade. Blooms early summer.	Air, or if still green, glycerine.

DRIED FLOWERS			
Name	Type/description	Cultivation/ Flowering season	Method of preservation
Helichrysum bracteactum Strawflower/ everlasting/ immortelle	Daisy-like, papery flowers in red, orange, pink and yellow. Grown as half-hardy annual.	Light or poor soil in full sun. Flowers in summer.	Air. Wire stem and head before drying.
Helipterum sp. Sunray/immortelle	Daisy-like, fragile flower. Red, rose pink and white. Hardy annual.	Light or poor soil in full sun. Flowers in summer.	Air
Hydrangea sp. Hydrangea 	Shrub with lacy flowerheads usually pink or purple-blue. Moderately hardy.	Rich, moist soil in semi or light shade. Best sheltered. Flowers summer into autumn.	Air dry, while allowing stem to be in a little water. Do not replenish, but allow to dry to a crisp feel.
Lagurus ovatus Hare's tail grass	Egg-shaped, silky grassheads are greenish to creamy white. Hardy annual.	Cultivated garden soil, preferably in sun. Blooms from mid- summer to first frost.	Air
Lavendula sp. Lavender	Fragrant grey- blue flowers in spikes on slender stems. Moderately hardy dwarf shrub.	Light, well-drained even poor soil in warm, sunny spot. Flowers late spring/summer.	Air
Limonium sp. Sea lavender	Profuse tiny flowers and ever- green leathery leaves. Blue, white or pink. Ultra-hardy perennial.	Well-drained, fertile soil. Good by the sea. Flowers mid – late summer.	Air
Limonium sinuatum *(Statice sinuata)* Statice	Sprays of yellow, pink, lavender, dark blue and white flowers.	Well-drained, soil in full sun. Usually grown as a half-hardy annual.	Air

DRIED FLOWERS			
NAME	TYPE/DESCRIPTION	CULTIVATION/ FLOWERING SEASON	METHOD OF PRESERVATION
Lunaria annua Honesty/silver dollar	Mauve flowers; flat, circular seedpods. Under the papery cover is a silvery disc. Hardy biennial.	Ordinary, well-drained soil. Will tolerate some shade. Flowers early summer.	Air dry seedpods. Then remove outer casing to reveal striking, pearly-looking discs.
Nigella damascena Love-in-a-mist	Saucer-shaped flowers in blue or pink. Thread-like bracts. Stripy green seedpods. Hardy annual.	Any good soil in sun or partial shade. Sow autumn or early spring. Flowers summer.	Dry seedheads by air.
Paeonia sp. Peony	see Fresh Flowers	See Fresh Flowers	Air/Desiccant
Papaver sp. Poppy	Bold, crepe-like, cup-shaped flowers. Usually red. Moderately hardy. Annual and herbaceous perennial types.	Dry, poor soil in hot sun. Flowers summer.	Dry seedheads by air.
Physalis alkekengi Chinese lantern/ bladder cherry	Bright orange, lantern-like calyces. Ultra-hardy perennial.	Well-drained, fertile soil in full sun. Flowers late summer.	Air
Rosa sp. Rose	see Fresh Flowers	see Fresh Flowers	Air/Dessicant
Solidago sp. Golden rod	Tiny yellow flowers in dense sprays. Ultra-hardy perennial.	Moist, well-drained, fertile soil in sun. Flowers late summer/autumn.	Air

PRESSED FLOWERS			
NAME	TYPE/DESCRIPTION	CULTIVATION/ FLOWERING SEASON	NATURAL SEASON
Alyssum saxatile Gold dust	Trailing rock garden plant with golden yellow flowers.	Well-drained soil in full sun.	Spring to mid-summer.
Centaurea cyanus Cornflower	see Fresh Flowers	see Fresh Flowers	Summer
Delphinium sp. Delphinium	see Fresh Flowers	see Fresh Flowers	Summer
Dianthus sp. Carnations/pinks	see Fresh Flowers	see Fresh Flowers	Summer
Filipendula sp. Meadowsweet	Tall, clump-forming plants with flat-top plumes of tiny flowers. Pink shades. Ultra-hardy herbaceous perennial.	Moist soil in sun or partial shade.	Summer
Iberis umbellata Candytuft	Clusters of white, red or purple flowers. Hardy annual.	Well-drained, moist soil in a sunny position.	Summer

PRESSED FLOWERS			
NAME	TYPE/DESCRIPTION	CULTIVATION/ FLOWERING SEASON	NATURAL SEASON
Lobularia maritima (*Alyssum maritimum*) Sweet Alyssum	Trailing rock plants with profuse white or pink flowers. Very hardy evergreen.	Well-drained, chalky soil in full sun.	Spring and summer.
Montbretia sp. (sometimes listed *Crocosmia sp.*) Montbretia	Bright orange arching spikes of trumpet-shaped flowers and sword-shaped leaves. Hardy corm.	Well-drained soil in full sun. Plant in spring.	From mid-summer.
Myosotis sylvatica Forget-me-not	see Fresh Flowers	see Fresh Flowers	Spring and early summer.
Narcissus sp. Daffodil/narcissus	see Fresh Flowers	see Fresh Flowers	Spring
Polyanthus (sometimes listed *Primula x polyantha*) Polyantha/primula	Primrose-type flowers. Wide colour range. Very to moderately hardy perennial.	Moisture-retentive, fertile soil.	Spring

PRESSED FLOWERS			
NAME	TYPE/DESCRIPTION	CULTIVATION/ FLOWERING SEASON	NATURAL SEASON
Potentilla sp. Cinquefoil	Saucer-shaped flowers and strawberry-type leaves. Usually shades of red and yellow. Very hardy perennial. There are also herbaceous perennial types.	Any soil in full sun.	Summer
Ranunculus sp. Buttercup	Bright yellow, waxy flowers. Very hardy perennial.	Moist soil in sun or light shade.	Late spring/ early summer.
Rosa sp. Rose	see Fresh Flowers	see Fresh Flowers	Summer
Sanguisorba minor (Poterium sanguisorba) Salad burnet (Garden burnet)	Reddish-brown stems grow up through leaves, and greenish-red, globular flowers appear at top. Widely grown as a medicinal herb.	Prefers lime soil. In sun or partial shade.	Spring – autumn
Viola sp. Pansy	Asymmetrical round flowers in wide colour range, often bicolour with dark centre. Short-lived perennial treated as hardy annual or half-hardy biennial.	Moist, fertile soil in sun or semi-shade. Good patio, bedding and edging plant.	Summer
Viola tricolor Heart's ease	Tiny pansy, usually cream, yellow or purple-red. Hardy perennial.	Moist soil. Sun or partial shade.	Summer

EDIBLE FLOWERS			
NAME	TYPE/DESCRIPTION	CULTIVATION/ FLOWERING SEASON	NATURAL SEASON
Anthemis nobilis Chamomile	White daisy flowers with yellow eyes.	Light, sandy soil in sunny position.	Summer
Borago officinalis Borage	Coarse, hairy leaves with clusters of deep blue star-shaped flowers. Hardy annual.	Well-drained soil in sun. Sow in early spring.	Summer
Calendula officinalis Marigold	Bright orange/ yellow daisy-like flowers. Hardy annual. Use the single-flowered, pot marigold for cooking.	Most garden soils in a sunny position. Sow early spring.	From early summer through to end of year if climate mild.
Dianthus sp. Carnations/pinks	see Fresh Flowers	see Fresh Flowers	Summer
Lavendula sp. Lavender	see Dried Flowers	see Dried Flowers	Late spring/summer.
Mentha sp. Mint	Fragrant spear-shape leaves in a variety of scents and tastes. Rampant growth.	Moist and dank conditions in sun or shade.	n/a

EDIBLE FLOWERS			
NAME	TYPE/DESCRIPTION	CULTIVATION/ FLOWERING SEASON	NATURAL SEASON
Pelargonium sp. Scented geranium	Highly fragrant leaves with small, usually pink/white flowers. Tender evergreen plants.	Well-drained soil. Likes to be grown from cuttings in pots.	Summer
Primula sp. Primrose	Rosette plants with five-petalled flowers. Yellow, pink and purple. Very hardy.	Moisture-retentive soil and some shade.	Spring and early summer.
Rosa sp. Rose	see Fresh Flowers. Both petals and rose hips can be used in recipes.	see Fresh Flowers	Summer
Thymus sp. Thyme	Aromatic dark green leaves with clusters of mauve flowers.	Well-drained, fertile soil in sun. Replace after 3-4 years.	Summer
Tropaeolum majus Nasturtium	Bright orange/ yellow flowers. Hardy perennial.	Ordinary or poor soil in a sunny position. Sow in spring.	Summer
Viola odorata Sweet violet	Tiny purple flowers. Hardy perennial.	Rich, moisture-retentive but well-drained soil, shielded from fierce sun.	Spring

SCIENTIFIC CLASSIFICATION

The following is an alphabetical list of common names of plants used in this book and their Latin equivalents.

Common name	Latin name
Agrimony	Agrimonia
Alstroemeria	Alstroemeria sp.
Alyssum, sweet	Lobularia maritima (Alyssum maritimum)
Amaryllis	Hippeastrum sp.
Anemone	Anemone sp.
Astrantia	Astrantia sp.
Baby's breath	Gypsophila paniculata
Basil	Ocimum basilicum
Bay, sweet	Laurus nobilis
Beard grass	Polypogon
Bells of Ireland	Molucella laevis
Bergamot	Citrus aurantium bergamia
Bird of paradise	Strelitzia reginae
Borage	Borago officinalis
Bottlebrush	Callistemon sp.
Bouvardia	Bouvardia sp
Buchu	Agathosma crenulata
Bulrush	Scirpus sp.
Bupleurum	Bupleurum sp.
Burnet, salad or garden	Sanguisorba minor (Poterium sanguisorba)
Buttercup	Ranunculus sp.
Buxifolium	Leiophyllum buxifolium
Canary grass	Phalaris canariensis
Candytuft	Iberis umbellata
Carnation	Dianthus caryophyllus
Catmint	Nepeta
Chamomile	Chamaemelum nobile
Chervil	Anthriscus cerefolium
Chicory, wild	Cichorium intybus
Chincherinchee	Ornithogalum thyrsoides
Chinese lantern	Physalis alkekengi
Chive	Allium schoenoprasum
Clematis	Clematis sp.
Clubrush	Scirpus sp.
Cornflower	Centaurea cyanus
Cotton lavender	Santolina chamaecyparissus
Cow parsley	UK: Anthriscus sylvestis USA: Heracleum lanatum
Cowslip	Primula veris
Daffodil	Narcissus sp.

Common name	Latin name
Daisy	Bellis perennis
Daylily	Hemerocallis sp.
Elderflower	Sambucus nigra
Endive	Cichorium endivia
Eryngo	Eryngium sp.
Everlasting	Helichrysum bracteatum
Feverfew	Chrysanthemum parthenium
Forget-me-not	Myosotis sylvatica
Foxglove	Digitalis sp.
Frisée (endive)	Cichorium endivia
Garlic, ornamental	Allium sp.
Geranium	Pelargonium sp.
Gerbera	Gerbera jamesonii
Globe artichoke	Cynara scolymus
Golden rod	Solidago sp.
Grape hyacinth	Muscari sp.
Gypsophila	Gypsophila paniculata
Hare's tail grass	Lagurus ovatus
Heart's ease	Viola tricolor
Hellebore	Helleborus sp.
Holly	Ilex aquifolium
Honesty	Lunaria annua
Honeysuckle	Lonicera sp.
Hop	Humulus lupulus
Hyssop	Hyssopus officinalis
Immortelle	Helichrysum bracteatum Helipterum roseum Xeranthemum annuum
Ivy	Hedera sp.
Jasmine	Jasminum sp.
Jonquil	Narcissus jonquilla
Knapweed	Centaurea
Lady's mantle	Alchemilla mollis
Larkspur	Delphinium consolida
Laurel, common or English	Prunus laurocerasus
Laurustinus	Viburnum tinus
Lavender	Lavandula angustifolia
Lemon balm	Melissa officinalis
Lemon mint	Mentha x piperita citrata
Lemon verbena	Lippia citriodora

Common name	Latin name
Lilac	Syringa sp.
Lily	Lilium sp.
Lily-of-the-valley	Convallaria majalis
Lobelia	Lobelia erinus
Lotus	Nelumbo lucifera
Love-in-a-mist	Nigella damascena
Love-lies-bleeding	Amaranthus caudatus
Maidenhair fern	Adiantum capillus-veneris
Maple	Acer sp.
Marguerite	Chrysanthemum frutescens
Marigold, pot	Calendula officinalis
Marjoram	Origanum marjorana
Meadowsweet	Filipendula ulmaria
Medick	Medicago falcata
Melilot	Melilotus altissima
Mimosa	Acacia sp.
Mint	Mentha sp.
Mock orange	Philadelphus sp.
Montbretia	Montbretia sp (Crocosmia sp.)
Nasturtium	Tropaeolum majus
Nipplewort	Lapsana communis
Oak, English	Quercus robur
Oats	Avena sp.
Onion, ornamental	Allium sp.
Oregano	Origanum vulgare
Pansy	Viola sp.
Pearl everlasting	Anaphalis sp.
Pennyroyal	Mentha pulegium
Peony	Paeonia lactiflora
Persian buttercup	Ranunculus asiaticus
Peruvian lily	Alstroemeria sp.
Pincushion flower	Scabiosa stellata
Pink	Dianthus x allwoodii
Poppy	Papaver
Potentilla	Potentilla sp.
Primrose	Primula vulgaris
Pulmonaria	Pulmonaria sp.
Quaking grass	Briza maxima
Queen Anne's lace	UK: Didiscus caeruleus USA: Daucus carota
Rock rose	Cistus
Rose	Rosa sp.
Rosemary	Rosmarinus officinalis
Rue	Ruta graveolens

Common name	Latin name
Safflower	Carthamus tinctorius
Sage	Salvia officinalis
Sandflower	Ammobium sp.
Scabious	Scabiosa stellata
Sea holly	Eryngium oliverianum
Sea lavender	Limonium sp.
Scented geranium	Pelargonium sp.
September flower	Aster sp.
Shepherd's purse	Capsella bursa-pastoris
Silver dollar	Lunaria annua
Silverweed	Potentilla anserina
Snow-on-the-mountain	Euphorbia marginata
Snowball flower	Viburnum opulus
Southernwood	Artemisia abrotanum
Spiraea	Spiraea sp.
Sprengeri fern	Asparagus sprengeri
Spurge	Euphorbia sp.
Statice	Limonium sinuatum
Strawflower	Helichrysum bracteatum
Sumach	Rhus typhina
Summer cypress	Kochia scoparia
Sunray	Helipterum roseum (Acroclinium roseum)
Sweet pea	Lathyrus odoratus
Tansy	Tanacetum vulgare
Teasel	Dipsacus sativus (Dipsacus fullonum)
Thyme	Thymus sp.
Tulip	Tulipa sp.
Venus's hair	Adiantum capillus-veneris
Vetch	Vicia sativa
Violet, sweet	Viola odorata
Viola	Viola
Virginia creeper	Parthenocissus quinquefolia
Water dropwort	Oenanthe fistulosa
Wheat	Triticum aestivum
Wild carrot	Daucus sp.
Winged everlasting	Ammobium sp.
Winter savory	Satureja montana
Witch hazel	Hamamelis sp.
Wood avens	Geum sp.
Xeranthemum	Xeranthemum annuum
Yarrow	Achillea sp.

INDEX